I Took a Lickin' and Kept on Tickin' (And Now I Believe in Miracles)

I Haven't Understood Anything Since 1962 and Other Nekkid Truths

You Can't Put No Boogie-Woogie on the King of Rock and Roll

If I Ever Get Back to Georgia, I'm Gonna Nail My Feet to the Ground

Don't Forget to Call Your Mama . . . I Wish I Could Call Mine

Does a Wild Bear Chip in the Woods?

Chili Dawgs Always Bark at Night

Don't Bend Over in the Garden, Granny, You Know Them Taters Got Eyes

When My Love Returns from the Ladies Room, Will I Be Too Old to Care?

My Daddy Was a Pistol, and I'm a Son of a Gun

Shoot Low, Boys, They're Ridin' Shetland Ponies

Elvis Is Dead and I Don't Feel So Good Myself

If Love Were Oil, I'd Be About a Quart Low

They Tore Out My Heart and Stomped That Sucker Flat

Don't Sit Under the Grits Tree with Anyone Else But Me

Won't You Come Home, Billy Bob Bailey?

Kathy Sue Loudermilk, I Love You

Comedy Albums

On the Road with Lewis Grizzard

Lewis Grizzard Live

Let's Have a Party

Addicted to Love

Don't Believe I'da Told That

From Moreland to Moscow

IT WASN'T ALWAYS EASY, BUT I SURE HAD FUN

GRIZZARD

IT WASN'T ALWAYS EASY, BUT I SURE HAD FUN

The Best of Lewis Grizzard

VILLARD BOOKS • NEW YORK • 1994

Portions of this book were originally published in *I Took a Lickin' and Kept on Tickin' (And Now I Believe in Miracles); I Haven't Understood Anything Since 1962 and Other Nekkid Truths; You Can't Put No Boogie-Woogie on the King of Rock and Roll; If I Ever Get Back to Georgia, I'm Gonna Nail My Feet to the Ground; Chili Dawgs Always Bark at Night; Don't Bend Over in the Garden, Granny, You Know Them Taters Got Eyes; When My Love Returns from the Ladies Room, Will I Be Too Old to Care?;* and *My Daddy Was a Pistol, and I'm a Son of a Gun,* all by Lewis Grizzard and published by Villard Books, a division of Random House, Inc., New York, and in Lewis Grizzard's syndicated newspaper column.

Library of Congress Cataloging-in-Publication Data
Grizzard, Lewis.
   It wasn't always easy, but I sure had fun : the best of Lewis Grizzard / by Lewis Grizzard.
     p. cm.
   ISBN 0-679-43831-9
   I. Title.
PN6162.G7834   1994
814'.54—dc20   94-18337

Manufactured in the United States of America
9 8 7 6 5 4 3 2
First Edition

Contents

4 Men: The Inside of My Tree House

5 Love: Azaleas in Bloom, Lizards in Need, and Marriages in Two Days Flat

6 Sex: The Urges That Hit You While Hanging Sheetrock

7 Culture: For Those Who Call Spaghetti Pasta

8 Media: A Local Yokel in Search of (Gasp) the Truth

9 Politics: Nuke the Gay Whales for Jesus

Foreword

DEDRA GRIZZARD

Living with Lewis Grizzard was often like living in one of his columns or books. The humor was ever present and never ending. So was the compassion. And the confusion and the anger and all the other things that made Lewis what he was.

I shared three and a half years of my life with this handsome rogue of a man, but only three days as his wife. In that time, I not only loved him, I came to understand him, and to see a side of him that few got to see—the side that *didn't* reveal itself in his writing.

He could irritate me—as it seemed he could irritate most of America—and he could break my heart, then lift my spirits and then inspire me and then make me laugh, all within a matter of moments. Even in the darkest days, when his health was really failing, Lewis could find things to laugh at. When told by his doctors that he had less than a fifty-fifty chance of surviving his last surgery, his immediate response was, "I just have one question: When's the next bus to Albuquerque?" During the last two weeks of his life in the hospital, he entertained the staff as well as his friends. That was his nature. While he could mourn for mankind in general, Lewis refused to ever mourn for himself.

While his public was delighted by Lewis's sense of humor, I was able to grow from it. He taught me to ignore trivial problems, to laugh at them. To Lewis, most problems were trivial. They were just a part of life that one had to deal with. One of his favorite phrases was "This ain't no dress rehearsal, honey." Perhaps those words, more than any others, describe how Lewis went through life.

He learned a few things from me, too, and I'm proud of that. He used to joke constantly about his inability to stay in a relationship. During his last days in the hospital, he wanted to talk about that. He told me, "I've finally figured it out, honey. A relationship isn't about winning—it's about *listening*." That's a side of Lewis not too many of his fans got to see—the side that was able to grow and evolve. We did a lot of growing in the short time we had.

Make no mistake, Lewis wasn't the easiest male on two legs to live with, but he was without doubt one of the most interesting. He did come with some baggage, too, not the least of which was that infamous four-legged male, Catfish. "Love me, love my dog" was never truer than in Lewis's case. I simply decided I got two for the price of one.

I came with some baggage, too: my daughter Jordan. Lewis not only accepted her, he loved her wholeheartedly and assumed the role of daddy as naturally as anyone could have hoped for. I think that much of his love for Jordan, and the way he treated her, came from his mother. I've learned to watch how a man treats his mother, because that's how he'll treat you. Well, to Lewis, Mama was the most important person in the world. She instilled in him all the values that enabled him to be a caring husband, father, and friend. His tenderness and compassion came directly from her. So did his work ethic and his sense of responsibility.

Despite his reputation, Lewis took great pleasure in the simple times he spent at home with me and Jordan. In his last year or so, we had many such quiet times. He took this time to reflect and to tell stories. I loved most the ones he would tell about his father, Major Grizzard. Lewis could make me laugh in one instant and then have me crying in my beer in the next.

I saw in Lewis a great desire to help others. He kept this generosity private, however. Few will ever know just how many individuals he helped both financially and emotionally. My goal is to preserve his memory in positive, caring ways, ways that will continue to assist those in need. A Lewis Grizzard scholarship has been established at the Journalism School at the University of Georgia (his greatest loves—after me and Jordan, I like to think—were the world of newspapers and that university, so this would please Lewis enormously). Another foundation is accepting donations in his name at Emory University School of Medicine for Cardiac Care. Lewis would have liked that, too.

Lewis Grizzard will be remembered for many things, some controversial, some comical, some sentimental. I will remember him as the greatest teacher I have ever known. I would like for his readers and fans to reflect upon the values Lewis stood for, values clearly seen and defined in this collection. The finest tribute Lewis could receive is for someone to extend a helping hand to another human being as a result of reading his words. That would please him more than any donation or foundation.

I feel his loss greatly. I have lost my knight in shining armor, my prince. I'm glad that I now have the opportunity to say thank you, Lewis, for the love you gave me and the memories we shared.

I know his readers and fans feel his loss, too. And to those readers I would also like to say thank you. Thank you for the prayers. Because of you I had him for one more year.

Introduction

STEVE ENOCH

Lewis McDonald Grizzard, Jr., was my best friend. I make no claims that I was his, but he was mine.

I met Lewis on the practice tee at the Melrose Club on Daufauskie Island, South Carolina, January 2, 1989. He asked me if I would join him in a round of golf. I did. Funny how eighteen holes of golf can change your life forever.

I had grown up playing with the likes of Lanny Wadkins and Curtis Strange; Lewis should have been a pushover. But, invariably, he rose to the challenge. He would never quit. He was many things to many people, but he was definitely the consummate competitor. Full of grit and determination, he would never concede defeat until a match was over. In that respect, he was more than my friend. He was my teacher.

Lewis, of course, had a mischievous irreverence that could delight and irritate fans and foes alike. Once, after a session in a bar in Williamsburg, Virginia, we made our way to the dining room, where the maître d' informed Lewis that coats and ties were required. In his best Southern drawl, Lewis stated flatly that he had neither. A bit nonplussed, the overseer of this gracious restaurant managed to produce the proper attire. Once again refusing to concede defeat, Lewis then told the maître d' that this was all well and good but, "I don't know how to tie a real tie." As all heads turned our way, Lewis patiently allowed this gentleman's gentleman to properly dress him. He was a master at striking good-humored blows at what he perceived to be "aristocratic airs."

I came to know him as a tenderhearted man, a man's man who would cry when Willie Nelson sang "Georgia on My Mind," for it reminded him so of his mother. He had been grounded in her love and stability and he missed her profoundly.

Eventually, we became partners, confederates, allies. We joined forces in many golf tournaments, amusements, and, ultimately, business endeavors. We had grown up very differently. I came from an affluent and stable Virginia family. Lewis came from rural Georgia. His parents divorced when he was six. By the time we met, his mom and dad were dead. Lewis had worked his way through school, from grammar school through his days at his beloved University of Georgia. Yet, as different as we were, we were both proud to be Southern and conservative, and we both felt as if the new politically correct world was leaving us behind. Today, they call it "bonding." To us, we'd simply become pals.

So many stories . . . so many episodes . . . so much life packed into a few short years. If laughter is the best medicine, Lewis was the medicine man.

I became vice-president and manager of Grizzard Enterprises. In both 1991 and 1992, Lewis did over a hundred lectures and performances. I traveled with him by plane, train, bus, taxi, and limousine. The laughter was endless and, often, so was the booze and conversation. We'd travel down the byways to the music of George Jones and Vince Gill while Lewis would denounce the ills of the world. Even in these diatribes, his humor abounded. Lewis was a master storyteller. He valued the simpler times, when people passed along their faith and heritage by telling stories.

One of my favorite stories—and I got to witness this one—occurred on a trip to Costa Rica. After his third heart surgery, Lewis informed me that he wanted to go there. "I hear it's beautiful, and I might want to move there someday if our society doesn't change." Upon our arrival, we headed straight for the hotel bar, where the party was in full swing. For the record, in the country of Costa Rica "ladies of the evening" are legal and abundant. Before we could even order a drink, one dark-haired beauty—clearly a pro—walked up to Lewis and in her sultry Spanish accent said, "You look so unhappy. For one hundred American dollars, I will do *anything* to make you happy." Lewis immediately looked skyward and said, "Thank you, Jesus." Then he handed her a crisp one-hundred-dollar bill and the key to his room and said, "Now go upstairs and write my Sunday column."

That's vintage Lewis.

My best friend died on March 20, 1994. Months have come and gone and I've done my grieving by telling "Lewisisms." I will pass through this mourning period by keeping the stories alive. That's why I know you'll enjoy this book: It keeps the stories alive. In a way—a most important way; perhaps *the* most important way—that keeps Lewis alive.

1 THE FAMILY

A Heritage of
Cheering Folks Up

In the Name of Jokes

The first forty years of being a Grizzard has been worth it, I think. I've had trouble with a world full of comedians thinking it was hilarious to mispronounce my name, but I have learned to deal with that. Grizzard is not the kind of name that is easily forgotten, either, and because the professor sat us in alphabetical order in a journalism course I had in college, I was able to sit next to the prettiest girl enrolled at the University of Georgia at the time because her name also began with a G. I never spoke to the girl the entire quarter because I was afraid to (I have some of my mother's people's blood in me, too, and her family was quite conservative). But when I was in the hospital following heart surgery, I received a get-well card from that very same girl and she said she remembered me quite well and reads the things I write. I could have kicked myself for not making some kind of move on her twenty years ago, but at least I now have her card acknowledging she actually knew I existed back then when I was sure she considered me—a skinny kid with thick glasses wearing high-water pants and white socks—a non-person.

Because I write books and newspaper articles that are attempts at being humorous, people often ask me where I got the ability to be funny.

That's easy. I got it from my daddy's side of the family. I got it from Daddy. Even at a very young age, I could tell the difference between my father's family and my mother's.

I love my aunts and my uncles and my cousins on my mother's side. My maternal grandparents raised me and I loved them with all my heart.

But they were quiet and spent a lot of time sitting under trees discussing the weather and who died recently. They were hard-working people, deeply religious, who warned me of the hellfire and of my streak of laziness that kept me from any interest in things I didn't enjoy doing, such as working in the fields where one tended to get very hot and dirty.

My mother's side of the family hated alcohol with a fierce passion. The Grizzards would take a drink and they would sing and they would dance and they would tell funny stories.

My daddy, even when his times were hardest, was never without a joke to tell some stranger he'd met thirty seconds earlier. I admit I am still stealing his material, still using characters that he forged first.

There was Lucille Wellmaker, a stout girl with whom my father went to school. She wore "bermuda-alls," overalls cut off at the knee, and carried a wagon spoke to dances. If anybody refused to dance with her, in my daddy's words, she would "turn the whole place out with that wagon spoke."

There was Hester Camp, who was uglier than an empty glass of buttermilk, and there was Ollie Groves, who used to ride a pig to school.

And there were his jokes. God, I still remember them, and

when I tell them again, often I fall into my father's voice. I do a magnificent impression of my father's voice:

There was this ol' boy who up and died, and he had loved to eat cheese all his life. His wife decided she'd put a big piece of Limburger cheese in the casket with him.

These two friends of his were looking down at the ol' boy in the casket and they didn't know about the cheese. One of 'em up and said, "Lord, Lord, he looks like he could just up and talk."

The other, gettin' a whiff of that two-day-old cheese, said, "If he did what I think he just did, he'd better say, 'Excuse me.'"

Then there were the two preachers:

There was this small town with a Baptist and a Methodist church. Both congregations had young preachers and they both rode bicycles to the services every Sunday morning, and every Sunday morning they would meet and exchange notes.

One morning, the Baptist preacher walked up on foot. The Methodist preacher said, "Brother, where is your bicycle?"

The Baptist preacher said, "Brother, I believe somebody in my congregation has stolen my bicycle."

The Methodist minister was appalled. He said, "I'll tell you how to get your bicycle back. You preach on the Ten Commandments this morning and when you get to 'Thou Shalt Not Steal' you bear down on it. You make 'em feel that fire, smell that brimstone! Whoever stole your bicycle will start feeling bad and bring it back to you."

The Baptist preacher said he'd try it. The next Sunday morning, sure enough, he was on his bicycle again.

"Hallelujah!" shouted the Methodist preacher. "I see you preached on the Ten Commandments and got your bicycle back. I'll bet you had the thief really squirming when you bore down on 'Thou Shalt Not Steal.'

"Well, that's not exactly what happened," said the Baptist minister.

"What do you mean?" asked the Methodist preacher.

"Well, I did preach on the Ten Commandments," his colleague said, "but when I got to 'Thou Shalt Not Commit Adultery,' I remembered where I left my bicycle."

He was a great people-watcher, my daddy. He saw funny where no one else would. He laughed at skinny, "wormy" men he'd see on the streets. Because the Grizzards were a rather large-in-the-waist group, whenever he'd see a fat woman he would say, "I believe there's one of the Grizzard girls." He never met a waitress he didn't call "Pearl."

Whenever he walked into a place to make a purchase and was not immediately waited on, he would offer up, in a loud, high-pitched voice, "I'm leav-*ing*." He once walked into a restaurant with a large appetite and noticed it said, "All the fried chicken you can eat, $3.95."

He called the waitress over.

"Pearl," he said, "is the management of this establishment prepared to back up this claim of all the fried chicken I can eat for $3.95?"

She said that it was.

"Then, dear woman," he said, "please alert the management that they are about to be in serious financial trouble."

The man could eat. God, how he could eat, especially after he returned from Korea, after nearly starving to death when his outfit practically was wiped out at Unsan. He'd been kept alive on rice for two weeks by a Chinese soldier who apparently wanted to desert. Years ago, I was much heavier myself, and my fat face looked even more like his than it does today.

He loved fried chicken. He also loved country ham and home-made biscuits and he used to buy those sausages he called "red-hots," which he would fry for a late snack. He ate what he called a "Snellville milkshake," cornbread soaking in a glass of butter-milk. One thing that was not passed down from my father to me was his affinity for buttermilk.

But I do have his voice. I also got his love for a funny story. And his love for great characters, great one-liners. I got his love of being the center of attention and with that the ability and material to have them rolling in the aisles.

I got his love for his country.

I am forty years old. I have been married and divorced three times and I don't have any children. The problem is that there was only one other male offspring from my father's family, and he is older than me, and he has only daughters, so if I do not come through with a son, then there is the distinct possibility the Grizzard name—or at least my father's family's use of it for quite a while—will end.

That is an awesome responsibility as I see it, and you know how those of us from the South can be about our family names.

I suppose I would like to have a son, or my ego would. I have fantasized about it over the years. I probably would name him Lewis McDonald Grizzard III. Maybe he would be known as "Little Lewis" and I would be "Big Lewis." We would go to ball games together and I would tell him stories like my father told me. And when he asked me about his grandfather, I would sit back and sigh and become wistful and say, "He was a great

American, son. You would have loved him, and he would have loved you."

Maybe he would grow up enjoying laughter and could pass it on to others. Maybe he would honor me, by using my material, as I have used my father's. Whatever talent I have, Daddy was the foundation of it.

Something like that would be nice to pass down a second time.

Legacy of the Love of Humor

The last of a special breed of folk is dead. There were twelve of them born to my paternal grandparents, Mama and Daddy Grizzard, of rural Gwinnett County, Georgia.

My father was the youngest. He's been gone twenty years. Aunt Nell was the oldest. She's been gone a long time, too.

Three of my late uncles were unforgettable characters. Walt and Wesley Grizzard were in the used-car business.

They had Grizzard Motors, and they were wily veterans of the trade. They were both big men with big voices, and very few customers escaped unsold when they stepped onto the lot.

"We're the walking man's best friend," my Uncle Wesley used to say.

My uncle Frank was a lawyer. My father took me to see him perform in the courtroom once. I was maybe twelve.

Uncle Frank was defending a man on a charge of making moonshine.

As he addressed the jury, a woman seated behind the defendant broke into hysterical tears.

Uncle Frank went into his client's military history, pleading with the jury to realize he had "fought on the bald hills of Korea."

And the woman sobbed on.

It took ten minutes for the jury to render a verdict of Innocent.

As we walked out of the courtroom, my father said to Uncle Frank, "That sure was pitiful about the man's wife."

"Wife?" Uncle Frank asked back. "What wife?"

"Your client's wife," said my father. "It sure was pitiful the way she cried."

"That wasn't his wife," said Uncle Frank. "It was just an old girl I paid fifty dollars to come here and squall."

The last of the twelve was my Aunt Rufie. She died last week in suburban Atlanta. She was eighty-four.

She and my father were close. My parents divorced when I was six, and when I would visit my father in Atlanta, we would usually wind up at Aunt Rufie's house.

Daddy would play her piano and sing. I loved that house because of the laughter that was always in it.

When my father fell on hard times during the last ten years of his life, it was my Aunt Rufie who stood by him the strongest.

"I could never turn my back on my baby brother," she often said to me when we talked of him after his death.

I'm going to be a pallbearer at Aunt Rufie's funeral. I will see some cousins I haven't seen in years. Death brings survivors together, regardless of how far they might have drifted apart.

The Grizzard men and women, my uncles and aunts, meant a lot to me when I was a child. I lived with my mother and didn't see them that often, but when I did, it was always a grand experience.

The legacy they left me was the love of humor. There wasn't a one of them who couldn't brighten a room, and I'm still stealing a great deal of their material.

A man came up to me a few years ago at a public gathering and said, "I grew up with your dad and all his brothers and sisters. When folks got down in Gwinnett County, they'd send for a Grizzard just to cheer them up."

That's my heritage. I couldn't be prouder of it.

The Night I Had It All

After I entered high school, I didn't visit Daddy nearly as often as I had when I was younger. There is a certain independence that comes with the high school years. I had a girlfriend, my mother's car most times I asked for it, and I had ball games. The need for Daddy had diminished somewhat, as it does for most who enter the teen years and change from a parent-dominated life to a life influenced mostly by peers.

I graduated high school in June 1964. Each student received

two seats for the graduation ceremony. Daddy appeared totally unannounced in Moreland at our house the afternoon before graduation night.

He hadn't been in Moreland since a few days after his return from Korea. I was shocked to see him. Mother was totally flustered. It had been years since they had seen each other.

He was as charming as ever. He was dressed immaculately with the bow tie. Always, the bow tie.

"I've come for my son's graduation," he said to Mother.

"How did you know it was tonight?" I asked him.

"A man should know what night his son is graduating from high school," he answered.

The immediate problem was obvious to me, if not to my mother. There were only the two seats. One for my mother. The other for my stepfather, H.B.

I was astounded at what I was thinking. I was thinking that Daddy hadn't bothered to show up for anything else in my life, and now here he was at my graduation, and he seemed to feel he could just tag along with the three of us.

Suddenly, for the first time in my life, I understood the position H.B. had been in ever since he married my mother. He always came in second to me in almost every situation that called for Mother's attention or affection. He obviously had been completely out of the running in any and every situation that involved Daddy and me. But he had endured it all, and a lesser man might not have.

And here on this night of all nights he would be sent to the back of the bus again. I could picture Daddy at the graduation, taking all the glory for his *mahvelous* son.

I feared there would be a fight. Daddy and H.B. had never met each other. What if it angered H.B. that Daddy was coming to our house? What if he insisted Daddy not go to the graduation?

Mother spoke first. She said, "Lewis, I don't know if it was a good idea for you to come here."

He looked surprised at that statement.

Then she went for the jugular.

"You've disappointed this child so many times. You've not been there when he needed you, or expected you. But tonight, you're here. I don't know if you deserve to see him graduate or not."

It stung him.

"I didn't want to be any trouble," he said. "I just wanted to see my son graduate high school."

Mother had a point, and so did he. But that didn't solve the problem of how H.B. would see all this.

"Do you want me to leave, Christine?" Daddy asked.

I was afraid she would say yes. I was also afraid she would say no. I wanted him there. I couldn't deny that. But I didn't want trouble. I didn't want feelings hurt. I could go and graduate high school alone if it came to that.

Mother hesitated before answering him. She couldn't bring herself to tell him to leave.

"H.B. will be home in a few minutes," she said. "We'll see what he says."

The three of us sat in the living room. The situation was completely awkward. Daddy tried to tell jokes. Mother and I laughed nervously. It would really be a lot simpler, I began thinking, if he would just bow out of this gracefully and there would be no confrontation with H.B.

He didn't, though. I had painted H.B. as a terrible ogre to him. I guess he wanted, if nothing else, to meet the man.

I felt guilty for what all I had said about H.B. and for the way I had treated him. There was the time he gave me the money to go to the Gator Bowl in Jacksonville with some of my friends when Mother had insisted he not do it.

There was the day I turned sixteen and went to get my driver's license. I had been marking off the days for a year. He drove me thirty miles to LaGrange to take the driver's test, and I had to show my learner's permit before I could take it. I hadn't known that. I didn't have my learner's permit with me.

It was Saturday. I had a date that night, my first where I drove the car. I was devastated by the news that I couldn't get my license.

H.B. drove me back to Moreland, then drove me *back* to LaGrange with my learner's permit. I got my license. He let me drive home. I kept my date. My life would have been temporarily ruined if I hadn't.

And he'd finally gotten off my back about the chores. He let me drink a beer with him occasionally. And eating the English peas at the father-son dinner hadn't been that awful of an experience, now that I thought about it.

H.B. drove into the driveway. I prepared for the worst. I am certain Mother did, too.

Daddy rose from his chair and walked toward H.B. as he opened the front door.

"I'm Lewis Grizzard," he said to H.B.

H.B. was startled for a moment. But he regained his composure and the two men shook hands. Mine were trembling.

"He's here for the graduation," Mother said, almost defensively.

"Well, good," H.B. said.

I couldn't believe he said that.

"I hope I'm not interfering," Daddy said. This was too good to be true.

But there remained the problem of the seats. I had only two. I finally spoke up.

"Daddy, we've only got two seats in the auditorium."

"I'll just stand in the back," he said. I hadn't thought of that. I felt a little better.

"No," said H.B. "I'll be glad to stand up. You and Christine are his parents."

For the first time, I saw my daddy rendered speechless. He finally spat out, "That's very kind, but you don't have to do . . ."

H.B. said, "I insist."

The three of them, my mother, my daddy, and my stepfather, drove to the graduation together in H.B.'s car. I drove my mother's. There was a party for the graduates at the Elks Club in Newnan after the ceremonies.

Daddy and Mother sat together while they passed out the diplomas. H.B. stood in the back.

I changed a great deal that night. I think more than anything else, I realized beyond any doubt that I had been fortunate to have a mother who stood by me and a stepfather who made her life better and who had put some stability—no matter how much I had rejected it—into mine.

I found Daddy with the principal of the high school when I came off the stage.

"You've done such a *mahvelous* job with our son," he was saying. "His mother and I appreciate it so much."

H.B. stood behind him with Mother and said nothing.

I went to my party. Mother said Daddy stayed in Moreland for about an hour and that he had been very gracious to H.B. for giving him his seat.

The graduation party was wonderful. My girlfriend gave me certain unexpected post-graduation liberties. Ronnie Jenkins and I iced down a case of beer in the back of the car, and we slipped out away from the dancing every now and then to have one.

I got home at eight the next morning, slept a few hours, and then left home for a summer job in Atlanta.

Driving away from Moreland, I sensed there never would be a night quite as fulfilling as the one that had just passed. For a few hours, I had it all.

Children Are Forever

Two very close friends of mine recently became fathers for the first time.

Another friend's wife is scheduled to deliver their first child soon.

All three of these men are forty or older.

"It's never too late," each has said to me at one time or the other during their wives' pregnancies.

I guess they're right. I'm forty-one, been down one time, two times, and three times in marriage, but as far as I know, I have held on to my ability to father a child.

We actually tried in my first marriage, but there was a problem she later overcame with medical help. Now, with her new husband, she is the mother she always wanted to be.

Second time was a whirlwind. Third time, she already had two, one out in the playroom screaming, the other outside riding his Big Wheel.

Ever hear the sound a Big Wheel—a plastic tricycle—makes as it is pedaled across a driveway?

Severe nervous breakdowns have been spawned from less.

"Men," a wise person once said to me, "often want children to satisfy their egos. They want to look down in that crib and say, 'Hey, that's my boy!'

"They look upon their children as proof of their manhood, and as their link with immortality, but some never quite understand the responsibility that comes with being a father to a child.

"It takes a real grown-up to be a good parent. And some men never really grow up."

I've thought about those words often, especially lately when previously childless friends suddenly turned faithful and multiplied.

Why would I really want a child? To satisfy my ego? To leave a living monument?

To have something I could love without conditions and be loved in return in the same manner? (That sort of thing is difficult to find, you know.)

In order to be the father I never really had? To be able to pass along what I have learned, what I think to be the truth and the way?

But a number of things stand between me and fatherhood. Number One being the fact I'm not married.

But even if I did marry again, I'd probably still think twice about children.

I've proved I'm not a good marriage risk. I came from a broken home. I don't want my child to have to do the same.

There remains childlike tendencies in my own repertoire. I have not quite given up on the idea of finding the ultimate party, and sometimes I have trouble giving up the night.

And there is the fact most things have an escape clause. You can leave a bad marriage, a bad job, and a city where the sun never shines. But children are forever.

What I could do rather than have children of my own is become the friendly uncle to my three buddies' children.

I could joke with them and bring them small gifts and enjoy their company while I am around them, and then split with no responsibility for them when the spirit moves me.

I'd miss the "goodnight, Daddy"s, but I also wouldn't have to put up with strange, loud music coming from the upstairs bedroom and explaining to my son if he didn't take off that earring, I would cut him out of the will.

This entire discussion, quite frankly, has made me nervous. Maybe I'll bring it up again next year.

Of Time and Birth

A friend of mine became a father for the first time last week. He's even older than I am.

Yesterday, we were sitting on the front porch of the fraternity house drinking beer. Today, he's got a son.

I remember what the old folks used to say: "Lord, where does the time go?"

I didn't understand them then. I do now.

So we talked about his kid.

"He's got more hair now than I do," said my friend, whose bald spot showed up four or five years ago.

"How big was he when he was born?" I asked.

"Eight pounds, eleven ounces. He's going to be a big 'un."

"Did you get to hold him right after he was born?"

"Yeah, I had to scrub up, and then I got to hold him. That's when I really realized I had a son. That's when the bonding really takes place between father and son."

We never talked about it, but I always assumed my friend had his heart set on a boy child.

He's an ex-jock who still is competitive as ever on a tennis court, the golf course, or in his den throwing darts.

He had a wild streak in him when he was younger, and a lot of lovely ladies stood by with broken hearts and watched him go.

He was the best dancer who ever shagged to "Stubborn Kind of Fellow" back in school. He drove a red 1950 Chevy convertible and voted for Barry Goldwater.

After school, he flew airplanes, went to a war, went into business, and built a home the size of a small town.

A man like that wants a son.

His wife wanted him in the room with her when she bore him his child.

"I guess you were pretty happy when you saw it was a boy," I said to him.

"It wasn't like that," he said. "My thoughts were more with my wife than with anything else. She was a trouper."

"You mean she was in a lot of pain?"

"Let me put it to you this way—if it were up to me and you to have babies, there wouldn't be very many around."

I was impressed with his concern for his wife taking precedence over anything else. Knowing him, knowing me, knowing how much a son would mean to him, and knowing the general insensitivity of most men, I sensed a friend entering another phase of his life.

One where a man comes to peace with himself, there's the wind to move him an inch, and he knows, without doubt, that in wife and child he has the only treasures that really matter anyway.

I used to laugh at such. Now, I'm jealous of it.

Lord, where does the time go?

It's Only Sheepskin Deep

Everyone worries about how much it costs to go to college.

I read a figure that said the cost of one year of schooling at prestigious institutions such as Yale and Harvard, and other places where the football teams never go to a bowl game, was twenty thousand dollars.

One female student interviewed on the Yale campus said, "I think it's worth it."

A Porsche is worth it at fifty thousand dollars, too, if Daddy's check is coming in each month.

It's been twenty years since I was in college, but I still feel I am qualified to offer a few suggestions to parents as to how to cut down on the price of educating their little spoiled darlings.

If you can't finance twenty thousand dollars a year on what you make in annual salary down at the plant, and your kid wants to go to Harvard because that's the best place to go if you want to meet, and perhaps later marry, a Kennedy, suggest alternatives.

"How about good ol' State U?" you might ask.

Your kid's eyes will roll back in his or her head, the classic teenage expression that means you have been completely out of touch with what's happening since the year Rome was sacked.

Then say, "Okay, I can't afford Harvard and you don't want to go to State U, but I can get you on the third shift at the plant." That should work. You wouldn't want your kid to meet and marry a Kennedy anyway. Those people probably wear ties at dinner.

Speaking of work, here's another way to cut down on what it costs to put your child through college.

Suggest he or she get a part-time job to help pay for some of the expenses. This suggestion likely will send your child into a fainting spell.

"But how," your daughter will ask, when she is revived, "can I work and still have time to be on the Homecoming Float Committee at the sorority house?"

Explain how you had to sell magazines door-to-door to put yourself through college, and if she doesn't get a job, there won't be enough money for sorority dues.

Your daughter will hate you, but only until her own children reach college age.

Here are some other ideas of how to cut the high cost of college:

1. Never send your children off to school with a convertible sports car or a credit card. The sports car will break down, and you will have to pay for it to be repaired.

   A college-age individual with a credit card will wear the writing off the plastic before Christmas break.
2. Don't allow your child to do anything because one of his or her friends is doing it—you sell used cars, the friend's dad is a television evangelist.

3. As soon as your child leaves for college, move to a new address and get an unlisted phone number so you won't be getting any letters or phone calls begging for money.

Some of these suggestions may seem cruel, but it's either use them or wind up spending a fortune on your kid's education and have him or her marry a Kennedy and when they come over for dinner you won't be able to eat in your shorts.

It's your decision.

Gift Ideas for Today's Teenagers

I hear a lot of my male friends complaining because they don't know what to give their children for Christmas.

Allow me to clarify that. The men I hear complaining the most are the ones with teenage children. Those with younger offspring appear to have it much easier.

They buy their kids Nintendo games and dolls that file sex-discrimination suits. These seem to have replaced the toy truck and Barbie.

But what do you give the teenager on the brink of the nineties? I would really like to help these people, but my credibility in this area, I admit, is somewhat suspect since I don't have any children, teenage or otherwise.

However, as an observer of life in all its phases, perhaps an outsider like myself can, in fact, select appropriate gifts for teenagers even better than their parents can.

I have already admitted I am not a parent, but I did have some. And in the immortal words of my mother, "Believe it or not, I was a teenager myself once, and I don't care if you are sixteen, you're not getting a Corvette for Christmas."

In other words, I think I can understand both points of view, thereby giving me an edge over parents whose minds are cluttered by such thoughts as, If I give my kid a Corvette for Christmas, will he (or she) drive it through a Kmart?

Here are some gift ideas for teenage boys:

- An earring: Earrings have become quite popular with teenage boys. I realize most fathers likely can't stand the thought of their sons wearing an earring, but they're cheaper than a Corvette and he's already dyed his hair orange.
- A guitar: What do you think you give a kid who wears an earring and dyes his hair orange? A set of golf clubs?
- A motorcycle: Maybe he'll drive it through a Kmart and get sent to reform school. You can tell your friends at the club your son has joined the Marines.
- A face-lift: As soon as a kid dyes his hair orange, starts wearing an earring, and joins a rock group, the term "zit-head" takes on an entire new meaning.
- A box of condoms: Believe or not, some chicks go for zitheads.

Now for your teenage daughter:

- Tight-fitting jeans: Daddy's little girl has grown up. Plus, all the other girls are wearing them.

- A pair of red high heels to wear with her tight-fitting jeans: What, you wanted to give her a chastity belt?

- A convertible: Perhaps she'll drive it through a Neiman-Marcus and get sent to girls' reform school, where she'll be safe. You can tell your friends at the club your daughter has become a nun.

- A trip to Europe: in case the convertible thing doesn't work. Maybe while she's gone, she'll forget about that zit-head she's been dating.

- A box of condoms: in case she doesn't.

Leading a Dog's Life

A great number of you have been kind enough to ask how my dog, Catfish, the black Lab, fared as the guest of honor at the recent First Annual Catfish Festival in Scottsboro, Alabama.

For those who might not have read earlier, Catfish's Aunt Louise drove him over to Scottsboro for the festivities, which was Catfish's first public appearance.

When Aunt Louise returned with him that evening, she couldn't wait to tell me.

"Your dog was wonderful," she said.

"He didn't embarrass me or the corporation?" I asked.

"Not in the least," she said.

You never know about a rookie at his first gig. He could have become nervous and bitten someone, committed an indiscretion during the parade, or chased the 4:15 Greyhound from Birmingham.

"He was a perfect gentleman," said Aunt Louise. "He let all the children pet him, he sat on command and never whined or barked once."

"Did the people seem to like him?" I asked.

"They loved him. He got to ride in a police car with the siren on, he appeared on two television shows, and they gave me a key to the city with his name on it."

This could be the start of an entire new career for Catfish.

Previously, by trade, he's been a shoe chewer, door scratcher, and a squirrel chaser.

He grew out of his shoe chewing and now has his own door through which he comes and goes as he pleases.

He has remained ever vigilant on squirrel patrol, however. Every day of his life, he chases squirrels.

He's never come close to catching one because they all run up trees, but doggedly, if you will, he continues his efforts.

But where might his new public career take him?

To other such festivals, of course. Also to shopping-center openings; used-car sales-o-ramas, Moose Club barbecues, and perhaps even to a hog-calling contest or at least a rat killing.

After that perhaps he could catch on with a beer company like those other dogs, or appear in a dog food commercial.

(On second thought, I hate dog food commercials. We all know the dogs are starved when they finally get a bowl of dog food put in front of them, and how does Ed McMahon know Alpo tastes all that good? Has he ever eaten any of it?)

At the moment, I'm also talking to Carson and Letterman. Earl Carson and Marvin Letterman, two guys who want Catfish to appear at the annual Red Bug Roundup in Itchlikehell, West Virginia.

I'm also negotiating with a man who wants Catfish to become national spokesdog for Sooper Dooper Doggie Scooper. A product dog owners especially need, lest our sidewalks become unwalkable.

I do intend, however, to bring Catfish along slowly. Too much too soon is a dangerous thing. That's why I told him he could keep the cigar he came home smoking last night.

"But that gold chain," I said, "has got to go."

He Up and Died and Broke My Heart

My dog, Catfish, the black Lab, died Thanksgiving night.

The vet said his heart gave out.

Down in the country, they would have said, "Lewis's dog up and died."

He would have been twelve had he lived until January.

Catfish had a good life. He slept indoors. Mostly he ate what I ate. We shared our last meal Tuesday evening in our living room in front of the television.

We had a Wendy's double cheeseburger and some chili.

Catfish was a gift from my friends Barbara and Vince Dooley. Vince is the athletic director at the University of Georgia. Barbara is a noted speaker and author.

I named him driving back to Atlanta from Athens, where I had picked him up at the Dooleys' home. I don't know why I named him what I named him. He was all curled up in a blanket on my backseat. And I looked at him and it just came out. I called him "Catfish."

I swear he raised up from the blanket and acknowledged. Then, he severely fouled the blanket and my backseat.

He was a most destructive animal the first three years of his life. He chewed things. He chewed books. He chewed shoes.

One day he went to my closet and chewed up my best pair of Guccis.

Catfish chewed television remote-control devices. Batteries and all. He chewed my glasses. Five pairs of them.

One day, when he was still a puppy, he got out of the house without my knowledge. The doorbell rang. It was a young man who said, "I hit your dog with my car, but I think he's OK."

He was. He had a small cut on his head and he was frightened, but he was otherwise unhurt.

"I came around the corner," the young man explained, "and he was in the road chewing on something. I hit my brakes the second I saw him."

"Could you tell what he was chewing on?" I asked.

"I know this sounds crazy," the young man answered, "but I think it was a beer bottle."

Catfish stopped chewing while I still had a house. Barely.

He was a celebrity. I spoke recently in Michigan. Afterwards a lady came up to me and said, "I was real disappointed with your speech. You didn't mention Catfish."

Catfish used to get his own mail. Just the other day the manufacturer of a new brand of dog food, with none other than George Jones's picture on the package, sent Catfish a sample of its new product. For the record, he still preferred cheeseburgers and chili.

Catfish was once grand marshal of the Scottsboro, Alabama, "Annual Catfish Festival." He was on television and got to ride in the front seat of a police car with its siren on.

He was a patient, good-natured dog, too. Jordan, my friend's daughter, who is five, has been pulling his ears since she was two. She even tried to ride him at times. He abided with nary a growl.

Oh, that face and those eyes. What he could do to me with that face and those eyes. He would perch himself next to me on the sofa in the living room and look at me.

And love and loyalty would pour out with that look, and as long as I had that, there was very little the human race could do to harm my self-esteem.

Good dogs don't love bad people.

He was smart. He was fun. And he loved to ride in cars. There were times he was all that I had.

And now he has up and died. My own heart, or what is left of it, is breaking.

2 ON THE JOB

The Toughest Suhbitch
I Ever Loved

Baptist Baseball and My First Big Break

Some might tell a youngster that he doesn't have to pick a career until he's older, but that's wrong. The earlier you decide what you are going to do in life, the bigger head start you get in pursuit of same.

My father had been a soldier, but I didn't want to be a soldier. All that marching. My mother was a schoolteacher, but I didn't want any part of that, either. Imagine having to go to school every day for your entire life.

I toyed with the idea of driving a train for a while. The Crescent Limited ran through Moreland between Atlanta and New Orleans on the Atlanta and West Point Railroad, and it seemed all the guy who drove the train had to do was sit there and blow the horn. I mean, you didn't have to learn a lot about steering.

After that, I considered opening a truck stop. The only businesses Moreland had was the knitting mill, Cureton and Cole's store, Bohannon's Service Station, Johnson's Service Station and Grocery Store, the Our House beer joint, and Steve Smith's truck stop.

A boy could learn a lot in a place like Steve Smith's truck stop. Steve was sweet on my mother, I think, and before she remarried (another guy), she would take me down to Steve's for a cheeseburger. We'd sit in one of the booths, and I'd eat while Steve and my mother would talk.

Among the wonders I saw at Steve's was a pinball machine that truckers would pour dime after dime into. I didn't know it at the time, but Steve paid off on the pinball machines. Let's say you aligned three balls, you won twenty free games. Steve paid a dime for each free game. The more dimes you put into the machine, the more free games you would win. Legend had it a man driving for Yellow Freight scored two thousand free games one night and won two hundred dollars. That legend brought truckers in by the droves, and Steve was just sitting there talking to my mother getting rich while truckers fed his pinball machine because of the two-thousand-free-game rumor. Advertising, false or otherwise, pays.

There was also one of those beer signs in Steve's where the little strands of color danced across the sign.

"How does that work?" I asked Steve one night.

"It's magic, kid," he said, and went back to talking to my mother.

I went to the rest room one night at Steve's and noticed a strange machine on the wall. There was a place to put a quarter for what was described on the machine as a "Ribbed French-Tickler—Drive Her Wild."

My mother wouldn't allow me near the pinball machines, but here was my chance to do a little gambling on my own. I happened to have a quarter, which I put in the slot. Lo and behold, I won. I received a small package and immediately opened it. There was a balloon inside. I filled it with air, tied a knot on the end, and walked out with it.

"Look, Mom," I said. "I put a quarter in the machine and got this balloon."

"Gimme that," said Steve, trying to take my balloon away. He ordered the waitress to bring me another Coke. In addition to the balloon, I also got a Coke out of the deal, so I figured the quarter had been well invested.

After the urge to open a truck stop when I grew up passed, I even had a brief flirtation with the idea of becoming a minister. My grandmother was always talking about her sister's boy, Arnold, who "made a preacher."

I wondered, how hard could it be being a preacher? You figure there's Wednesday night prayer meeting, then the Sunday service. Throw in a few weddings and funerals here and there, and that's about it. Also, somebody would always be trying to get you over to their house to eat, and nobody serves anything bad to eat to preachers. Plus, you'd never have to cut your own grass.

Only a few days into my thoughts of becoming a minister, however, an older cousin explained to me a minister wasn't allowed to do all the things I was looking forward to doing when I became an adult. Namely, drinking, smoking, cussing whenever you wanted to, and, since by that time I had learned what the balloon in the machine at Steve's truck stop was all about, I figured preachers likely would be denied that little pearl, too. I got off the minister thing in a hurry.

Uncle Grover couldn't read. But each day when he and Aunt Jessie left the mill to drive home for lunch, a quarter-mile away, they would stop by the post office, which was next to the knitting mill. There they would stop to pick up their mailed morning edition of the *Atlanta Constitution* and bring it home with them at lunch. Atlanta was a lot farther from Moreland back then than it is now.

When I was ten, it was at least five thousand miles to Atlanta, because I knew my chances of ever getting there were quite slim. Today, it's thirty-five minutes by interstate. My grandmother's yard looks a lot smaller to me when I see it now, too, so you know what time does to a lot of things. Shrinks them.

By the time I was ten, my brain was well on its way to being consumed by baseball. A lot of boys are like that, of course, but I may have gone to extremes heretofore unachieved. I never actually ate a baseball, or any other piece of baseball equipment, but I did sleep with the baseball my grandfather gave me for my birthday, and probably the only reason I didn't eat it was I knew my grandfather certainly was not a man of means and might have had a difficult time replacing it with any sense of dispatch.

There was a marvelous baseball team in Atlanta when I was ten. They were the Atlanta Crackers. For years, I thought they were named the Crackers because they had to do with, well, crackers.

Later, I would learn that the term came from the fact that Georgians were bad to carry around whips in the days of Jim Crow and slavery. And whips go "crack," and, thus, the name of the ball team. But at ten, in 1956, my world was an almost totally isolated one, and I finally decided the name had something to do with saltines, but I didn't have time to figure out exactly why or how.

Uncle Grover bought the first television set in Moreland. When word got out, people came from as far away as Grantville, Luthersville, and Corinth to get a glimpse of Uncle Grover's and Aunt Jessie's amazing box. It had about an eight-inch screen, if I recall correctly, and you had to sit real close if you wanted to see any detail, such as whether or not someone on the screen actually had a head. The adults would watch John Cameron Swayze on the national news, and Vernon Niles, who claimed to be his second cousin from Corinth, would always say, "If that's John Cameron's head, I've seen better hair on fatback."

It was the broadcasts of games on that television that summoned me first to the Crackers, but it was that copy of the *Constitution* Aunt Jessie and Uncle Grover brought home each day at noon that sustained my interest and affection. And one day, when I was reading of a Cracker sweep of a doubleheader in faraway Little Rock, it finally occurred to me:

The guy who wrote the story I was reading got to go to all the Cracker games, home and away, and ride trains, and actually got paid for doing it. What a revelation! My life set its course at that very moment.

I would be a sportswriter! Wasn't I sitting in my aunt's living room with my grandmother as she watched *TV Ranch,* and didn't I arise and declare, "Mama Willie! I've decided I want to be a sportswriter!"

And did she say, "Hush, Boots and Woody are about to sing 'Beulah Land,' " or did she say, "So that means you're not going to make a preacher?," or did she ask, "What's a sportswriter?"

I honestly can't remember, but from that day I had but one ambition, and that was to be the guy who covered the Atlanta Crackers, home and away, rode trains, and got paid for it.

There was something about that newspaper. Something that said to me it knew everything that was happening in the whole world but would kindly share it with me.

I cannot describe the anticipation I felt during the summers as I waited for Uncle Grover to drive into his driveway in the Pontiac with that paper.

I would begin my daily paper watch about eleven-thirty. It would seem a lifetime until a few minutes from noon when I would see Uncle Grover's Pontiac heading down the street.

Aunt Jessie usually held the paper, while Uncle Grover drove the car. She would never make it into her house with the paper, however. I would meet her as she stepped out of the car, and she would hand over that precious folding of newsprint.

I must mention *The Atlanta Journal* here, as well. The *Constitution* and the *Journal* were both owned by the Cox family of Ohio. The *Journal* was the afternoon paper.

My friend Bob Entrekin's father took the *Journal*, which I always read when I went to visit my friend.

I didn't understand how newspapers worked at that point, and I thoroughly enjoyed the *Journal* because it had all the stories and box scores from night games that the early edition of the *Constitution* didn't have.

What I didn't know was the early edition of the *Constitution* closed before night games were finished, but the *Journal* didn't close until the next morning.

I also became quite fond of the *Journal* because the sports section included sports editor Furman Bisher's column. It was funny. It was biting. It was a daily treasure. I made up my mind that when I became a sportswriter, I would write like Furman Bisher, and if it ever came down to a choice, I would rather work for the *Journal* than for the *Constitution*. You have to work out the details of your career early.

The odd thing is, now that I look back, after making my decision as to what to do with my life, it really wasn't that difficult achieving it. Maybe it's because I was just lucky. Maybe it's because my decision was just so *right*. I don't really know. I do know that most everything that has happened to me afterward in the newspaper business has felt natural and that must mean something.

My first sportswriting job came when I was ten. Moreland and the surrounding hamlets had no organized Little League program, as they did in the county seat of Newnan, where the well-to-do, not to mention the pretty-well-to-do, all lived. Out in the county, we were not-well-to-do-by-any-means.

What happened when I was ten was that the Baptist churches in the county decided to start a baseball league for boys. I was a Methodist at the time, but I showed up at the very next Baptist baptismal and was immersed in the name of the Lord, as well as in the name of a nicely turned double play or a line drive in the gap between left and center.

I was a pitcher. When our coach asked me, "What position do you play?" I simply said, "I am a pitcher," and that was that.

It also occurred to me it would be a fine thing to have the results of our league printed in the local weekly, the *Newnan Times-Herald*, which always carried all sorts of news about the fancy-ass Newnan Little League, where all the teams actually had uniforms. They also got a new baseball for every game.

For the first time in my life, I attempted a phone deal. I called the editor of the paper and told him of my desire that he run results of my baseball league.

The *Times-Herald* did run bits of news from the outlying areas, normally in a column under a thrilling heading that read, "News from the Moreland Community," which would be followed by something along the lines of the following:

Mr. and Mrs. Hoke Flournoy were the guests of Mr. and Mrs. Lon Garpe at their lovely double-wide home, located in the Bide-A-Wee trailer park, Sunday afternoon. Iced tea was served and a watermelon was cut.

Miss Jeanine Potts visited her mother, Elvira Potts, this weekend. Jeanine is currently a student at the Kut 'N' Kurl beauty school in Macon. Jeanine said Macon is a nice place to visit, but she was having trouble meeting fellow Christians.

Hardy Mixon and his wife, Flora, have returned home after their vacation to Panama City, Florida. Hardy said he enjoyed the air conditioning in the motel, the Sun 'N' Surf, but that Flora made him turn it down because it made her feet cold.

Narkin Gaines caught a possum last week and promptly ate it.

Brother Sims, the Baptist preacher, brought us a lovely message Sunday morning at the worship hour concerning the coveting of thy neighbor's ass.

As it turned out, it wasn't that difficult a proposition talking the paper's editor into carrying the results of our games.

"You get 'em to us by Tuesday," he said, "and we'll have 'em in the paper on Thursday."

I had my very first sportswriting job. And the very first week, I ran into my very first journalism ethics problem. In Moreland's opener, I happened to no-hit Macedonia Baptist in a 14–0 rout in which Dudley Stamps hit three home runs.

We hosted the opening tilt ("tilt" being one of the first sportswriting clichés I ever learned—for some reason, "tilt" can be used as a replacement for "game," "contest," or "showdown"). At the field behind the Moreland school, which had no fences, Dudley hit three shots into the patch of kudzu in deep left, and by the time they found the balls, he was already back on the bench pulling on a bottle of Birley's orange drink.

I had results of other league games phoned in to me, but there wasn't much there in the Arnco-Sargent vs. Corinth, well, tilt. They had to end the game after four innings, with Corinth ahead, 11–7, when various cows from a pasture that bordered the ball field broke through a barbed-wire fence and into the outfield, which they left unfit for further play.

In the Grantville–Mills Chapel engagement (I was learning more clichés by the moment), the only thing that happened that was the slightest bit interesting was that a stray dog had wandered onto the field, chased down a ball that got through the Grantville defense, and tried to run away with it. The dog was finally caught by the Grantville shortstop, who would become the league's fastest man and most prolific scorer, but by that time, the dog had gnawed several of the stitches off.

Since that was the only ball anybody had, they had to finish the game with it, and by the end of the sixth inning, it resembled a rotten peach more than a baseball. The game ended in an 8–8 tie, and Jake Bradbury, who owned the dog, was told to keep it penned during future games.

Clearly, my no-hitter was the big news, but should the lead of my first sports story feature my own exploits?

Later, I would learn that journalism ethics were nebulous, to say the least, so I followed my developing nose for news and went with the following:

> Brilliant Moreland right-hander Lewis Grizzard, in his first start in organized baseball, baffled the visiting Macedonia Baptist nine Saturday afternoon with a no-hitter. Dudley Stamps, in a lesser role, had three home runs in the 14–0 romp.

Uncle Grover and Aunt Jessie also took the weekly *Times-Herald*. When they brought it home at Thursday noon, I opened it even before the *Constitution*. Besides, the Cracker game had been on television the night before, so I'd seen little Ernie Oravetz lead the Chattanooga Lookouts to an easy 9–4 victory.

I will never forget gazing upon my name appearing in a newspaper for the first time. In fact, my name appeared in the newspaper for the first time *three times*.

The headline read:

MORELAND'S LEWIS GRIZZARD
NO-HITS MACEDONIA 14–0

Then came my byline:

By Lewis Grizzard

Then came the lead of my story, "Brilliant Moreland right-hander Lewis Grizzard . . ."

I had also mentioned my heroic exploits to the lady who wrote the column about who had iced tea and watermelon with whom, in hopes she might also make mention of my no-hit game. But she said she ran out of space because there was so much to tell about the women's Bible class taking a trip to an all-night gospel singing in Grantville that featured LeRoy Abernathy and Shorty Bradford (known as "the Happy Two"), as well as the Sunshine Boys, the Blackman Brothers Quartet, and a little blind girl who sang "Just as I Am." There wasn't a dry eye in the house after that lineup.

Despite that, I still broke into organized baseball and sportswriting in a big way, and I would wonder afterward if there was a possibility I might play for the Crackers when I grew up and also cover the games and get paid by the *Constitution*.

My dream of pitching professionally, however, came to an abrupt end my senior year in high school. They bused those of us out in the county to Newnan High School.

It was my final game as a Newnan High baseball player. We were playing mighty Griffin. We led 3–2 in the bottom of the sixth when I faced the Griffin catcher, who, with two outs and the bases loaded, looked about twenty-five years old.

I had whiffed the Griffin catcher in two previous plate appearances with slow curveballs. Now I worked the count to two balls, two strikes. My coach called time and came to the mound.

"Grizzard," he said, "don't throw this guy another one of those slow curveballs. He's seen too many of them already."

What did he know? The slow curve was my out pitch. The slow curve to me was what a piano had been to Mozart, a rifle to Davy Crockett, a tank to George Patton.

The Griffin catcher dug in, and I delivered that tantalizing dipsy-do of mine.

Are you familiar with the term "hanging curveball"? Mine not only hung, it actually stopped directly over the plate and waited for the Griffin catcher to hit it.

After the game, which we had lost 6–3, I asked my left fielder, "Did you have any chance to catch that ball the Griffin catcher hit?"

He said, "No, but I did manage to get a brief glance at it as it was leaving the planet."

So, no offers of a professional contract or a college baseball scholarship were forthcoming, but I still had my dream of being a sportswriter. At least you didn't sweat as much up in the press box as you did down on the field actually playing the game.

The Write Type

A friend whose son wants to grow up and be a writer asked me what courses the young man should concentrate on in high school.

To answer, I had to look back to my own high school days.

Certainly biology hasn't meant diddly to me as a writer. I could dissect a frog with the best of them in high school, but it hasn't come up since.

Neither has algebra or geometry, and I knew they wouldn't at the time. I basically learned everything I need to know about mathematics in the third grade, when they taught me to multiply.

Two times four is eight, which is how many I need to write today so I can take a couple of weeks off and work on my upcoming novel, titled *Don't Get Near Mama, Sailor, She's Been Eatin' Navy Beans.*

Learning about ancient history hasn't benefited me. Who cares when Rome was sacked? It should have had a better offensive line.

And geography. There's a lot of sand in Saudi Arabia. I could have learned that later in life simply by watching U.S. Marines wishing for a cold beer as they wait for President

Bush to decide whether or not he's going to get some of them killed.

History. When I was interviewed for this job, nobody asked me anything about Rutherford B. Hayes.

They did teach me grammar and punctuation, but that's why we have editors.

What I finally decided was the most important course I took in sixteen years of schooling was typing.

I have used this skill practically every day of my professional life.

Mr. Sheets, the basketball coach, taught me typing my junior year of high school. Typing teachers usually don't get a lot of credit for molding our youth, but in my case I am certainly beholden to Mr. Sheets.

I'm not certain how many words I now have to my credit, but I type each of them. If you can't type, you're going to be in a helluva mess if you want to be a writer.

In the first place you can't get a job with a newspaper if you can't type. They're going to sit you down at a computer and ask you to produce, and I don't care how much you know about computers, if you can't negotiate the keyboard, nothing readable is going to appear on the screen in front of you.

Some authors, I am told, write out their books in longhand. That's because they never learned to type. If they had, they wouldn't be scribbling on a sheet of paper for months at a time, which can cause severe pain in the hands and fingers.

That's why Edgar Allan Poe wrote all that weird stuff. His hands and fingers were always hurting him. The pain became so intense he began to see talking ravens.

So I told my friend to tell his son to enroll in a typing class as soon as possible.

"But what about foreign languages?" he asked.

"Maybe he ought to learn a little Japanese," I said.

Our golf courses today. Our publishing industry tomorrow. It could happen.

That There Education

Mother began saving for my college education with the first paycheck she ever earned. She bought bonds. She put cash in shoe boxes and hid them in the back of her closet.

Having enough money to send me to college when the time came consumed my mother. Besides the bonds and the shoe-box cash, she kept a coin bank, bought day-old bread, sat in the dark to save on the electric bill, never had her hair done, quit smoking, and never put more than a dollar in the collection plate at church. She used some simple logic for not tithing the Biblical tenth: "If the Lord wanted me to tithe that much, he wouldn't have made college so expensive."

Mother had no problems with my intention to study journalism. She wouldn't have cared if I had studied chicken proctology at the School of Agriculture, just as long as I was enrolled.

As a matter of fact, my mother did have something to do with my interest in putting words on paper. My mother was on constant grammar patrol when I was growing up.

Going to school with children from poor, rural backgrounds, as I did, I often fell in with a bad-grammar crowd.

What follows is a glossary of the way a lot of words were mispronounced around me constantly:

"His'n" (his)
"Her'n" (hers)
"Their'n" (theirs)
"That there'n" (That one)
"You got air asack? (Do you have a sack?)
"I ain't got nairn." (No, I'm afraid I don't.)

Mother also disliked another common grammatical error of the times. Many of my friends would say, in referring to their parents, "Daddy, he went to town last night"; or "Mamma, she went with him, and they didn't bring us air a thang."

"There is no reason to say 'Daddy, he,'" my mother would remind me. " 'Daddy' is identification enough."

"Ain't," of course, was a hanging offense. You never got away with double negatives or the popular answer to "Have you done your homework?" "Yes, I done done it."

My mother did allow, however, certain words and phrases common to Southern speech that might not be able to stand a harsh review, in the strictest sense, of whether or not they were proper.

My mother, for instance, had no problem with the use of the term "fixing" in place of "going to" or "it is my intention to," as in "I'm fixing to do my homework." I still say "fixing," and anybody who doesn't like it can stay in Boston and freeze.

My mother also had no problem with certain Southern expletives, such as:

"Hot-aw-mighty" (God Almighty)

"Dang-nab-it" (Of all the rotten luck)

"Dad-gum-it" (Same as above)

"Shut yo' mouth" (You're kidding me—and please note it's not "Hush yo' mouth," which a lot of people from up North think)

"Lawd, have mercy" (About the same as "Shut yo' mouth")

My mother would not abide, however, any form of swearing.

I never would have used the following words and phrases in this book if my mother were still alive, because it might have broken her heart. But she's gone now, and I suppose I can offer up such examples of common Southern curse words:

Shee-yet far (Southerners can probably say "shit" better than anybody else. We give it the ol' two syllable, "shee-yet," which strings it out a bit and gives it more ambience, if words can have ambience. "Shee-yet far" is Southern for "shit fire," which means something between "Oh, my God" and "Look out, Knute, she's headin' for the brier patch.")

Sumbitch (Southern, of course, for "son of a bitch." However, when people from the North try to say "sumbitch," it doesn't come out exactly right. Jackie Gleason tried to say it a million times in the immortal *Smokey and the Bandit* movies, but he never did pull it off.

I don't think Southerners actually say "sumbitch." It's more "suhbitch," as in "That suhbitch can flat play a cello," which I'm not certain has ever been said in the South, but I like to throw in such classy allusions like that to prove we've got more class than Yankees often give us credit for.)

Got-damn (You know.)

Ice (We don't say "ass" like other people do. I can't decide exactly how we say "ass," but "ice" comes rather close, as in "Shee-yet far, Randy, if that got-damn suhbitch don't watch his ice, somebody's goin' to break that cello right over his got-damn head.")

The term "ice" also brings up another interesting story about my mother. In the middle sixties the county schools of Georgia were integrated, and my mother wound up with a first-grade class made up mostly of black first-graders.

I almost forgot that "nigger" was taboo in my mother's house, too. In fact, my mother was the only person I knew who *didn't* say "nigger." She was the first person to explain to me that it was a derogatory term.

In those days, however, there were only three substitutes available for "nigger," all three of which are frowned upon by today's blacks and African-Americans.

The three substitutes were "colored," "knee-grow," and "nig-gra."

My mother never indicated to me which of the three substitutes she preferred, but thinking back, I'd think she preferred "knee-grow."

Although there remains the National Association for the Advancement of Colored People, "colored" brings to mind such phrases as "Colored Seat from Rear," a command one might have read on a bus or train in the fifties.

And people who used "nig-gra" always seemed to say that word with noticeable disdain. But "knee-grow," I think, was an effort on the part of some white people, like my mother, to also say, "The times they are a-changin', so let's get on with the program."

What concerned my mother (her students referred to her as "Miz Christine") most about the grammar of many of her black first-graders was their use of "axe" for "ask."

She attacked it this way:

She said, "Students, can you say 'asssssssss'?"

First-graders thought getting to say "asssssssss" at school was a riot.

After running through "asssssssss" several times, my mother would say, "Now, can you make the 'k' sound?," which, I suppose, is "kuh." Then Mother would say, "Put the two together: 'asssssssss-kuh.'"

Her methods might be attacked today as a manifestation of racial insensitivity. Blacks have every right to pronounce "ask" as "axe" if they want to, but a person who had been on constant grammar patrol for all those years must be given some forgiveness if her methods reeked of any sort of bias.

I made excellent grades throughout school. Again, if I hadn't, my mother would have inflicted both a verbal and physical beating upon me. My constant fear was "What if my mother saves up all that money for my college and I can't get in because I made a C in ancient history?" I hated ancient history because I didn't give a shee-yet when Rome was sacked, nor who won the Punic Wars. But because I didn't want to disappoint my mother, I studied and paid a fair amount of attention in class and made an A in ancient history anyway.

I applied to only one school, the University of Georgia. My high school counselor, one Mr. "Cheeks" Chandler, as he was affectionately known, told me Georgia's journalism school was one of the best in the country, right up there with the journalism schools at the University of Missouri and Northwestern.

I remember the day the letter came. It said on the front of the

envelope, "This is your official University of Georgia acceptance."

I gave Mr. Killingsworth, my employer at the bank, notice in
the middle of August. I went into his office and said, "Mr. Killingsworth, I have decided a career in banking is not for me. This
is my two-week notice."

He gazed up at the organizational chart to make certain I was
still at the bottom of it, so, I suppose, he could handle this with
a so-who-cares attitude. He didn't say, "Who cares?," but I
could see it on his face. What he did say was "Good luck, now
get back to work."

The Headline Hall of Fame

Frank Hyland was the best all-around talent who ever
worked for me. He could do it all. Report. Write. Edit. Lay out
the paper. Write wonderful headlines and photo captions. His
best headline came one morning when he sat on the rim quite
ill and quite green.

Peahead Walker was a character of the Southern sports
scene. He coached football in North Carolina and had a million
jokes and stories. Peahead was probably the most sought-after
sports speaker in the South in the late sixties. But Peahead died.
The *Constitution* carried the obit in the morning paper. The
headline had said something like:

COLORFUL PEAHEAD WALKER DIES

We had a Peahead obit, too. We had coded headlines at the *Journal*. I had ordered what was known as a K-3 on the Peahead story. A K-3 was one line of 36-point type, three columns wide, with an 18-point "kicker" above it.

You've seen kickers on headlines before. They look something like this:

<u>Tasted Good</u> (Kicker)
MAN BITES DOG (Headline)

Everybody on the rim took a shot at the Peahead headline, but none satisfied me. "It needs to say something about Peahead knowing a lot of jokes and stories," I said.

Frank opened his eyes and said, "Give the damn thing to me."

He wrote:

<u>He's Dead</u>
HAVE YOU HEARD THE ONE ABOUT PEAHEAD?

No way I could run it, but it sure went down in my Headline Hall of Fame.

In Search of a Pulitzer

They handed out the annual Pulitzer Prizes, journalism's highest awards, the other day, and once again I didn't get one.

It's becoming an all-too-familiar occurrence. Each year, I call my friends over, we ice down the beer and await the word from the Pulitzer committee.

Word never comes, but my friends drink all the beer I bought, anyway. How two people can drink that much beer is beyond me.

It's not like I haven't done anything to deserve the award. Twice last year, I wrote columns while suffering from a terrible hangover, and my crack investigative abilities enabled me to break a story that Colonel Oliver North and Indiana basketball coach Bobby Knight may be the same person.

The fact that I had never seen them photographed together was my first hint.

There were also columns that served the public interest. I was the person who first suggested that the surgeon general put out the word that smoking causes AIDS.

Smokers obviously aren't afraid of lung cancer, heart disease, emphysema or complications in pregnancy.

But threaten them with AIDS and, I firmly believe, that would pretty much do it for the habit of smoking.

And let us not forget my incisive piece that asked, "Will those oxygen masks really fall out in front of your face in an airplane in case there is a loss of cabin pressure?" Have you ever seen those oxygen masks do so? Do you know anybody who has? I rest my case.

And what about my biting commentaries?

What other journalist last year questioned whether or not an alligator can outrun a duckbill platypus?

Or who wondered why Jesse Jackson's forehead is so big and always seems to be perspiring?

Or why service stations keep their cash registers open and lock their bathrooms?

And what about the story I broke that Vanna White flunked spelling in the fourth grade?

Or that Johnny Carson lost his ability to speak eleven years ago? Or the fact that Ed McMahon is one of the world's most accomplished ventriloquists?

And what about my twenty-six-part series of columns that asked: "Turning right on red: friend or foe?"

Also, there's the fact that I could put the $3,000 that comes with the Pulitzer Prize to a lot of good uses. I need a new set of tires, the icemaker in my refrigerator is busted, I owe a couple of hundred from the gin game the other night, and I'm in desperate need of some new undershorts.

I suppose I'm so sensitive about not winning the Pulitzer again because it brings back the memories of never getting the pony I wanted for Christmas, the trip to Europe after graduation, or a date with the redheaded cheerleader.

Still, there's always next year and another round of Pulitzers. I can wait. I just hope my undershorts can, too.

3 WOMEN

Kathy Sue Loudermilk, I Miss You

The Tree House Syndrome

SOMEWHERE IN SOUTH FLORIDA—There is this place. I can't tell you the name of it or exactly where it is, but there is this place in South Florida where they have figured out the problem of women on the golf course.

I don't have any problem with women playing a little golf occasionally, but I always have thought it would be better if women had their golf courses and men had theirs.

That way, women could take their sweet time getting around the course, and if they happen to shoot 140, no big deal.

Before I catch the wrath of the female golfing populace, allow me to say upfront there are women who are much better golfers than me.

My problem is with the high-handicap woman golfer who will not pick up her ball and move on to the next hole once she's hit it fifteen or sixteen times and it's still not in the cup.

There are many slow men players, too, but men understand that once you reach double-bogey, there's no sense in frustrating yourself any further, so it's onward to the next tee.

But about this place: The reason I'm not going to put a name or location on it is that some flared-nostril feminist might read this and decide to file suit, and I might never be invited back as a guest.

Quite obviously, the place is a golf club. But not only are women forbidden from playing the course—under any circumstances whatsoever—they aren't even allowed on the grounds except once a year.

For the annual Christmas party.

Your wife drives you to the club. She lets you off at the front gate. Even phone calls from women are discouraged.

"And you can play gin rummy naked," a member explained to me.

I'm not certain I'd want to play gin rummy naked, but I saw the member's point.

There aren't any women within miles of the club, so you're safe to belch or curse or make funny noises with your armpit or, if you so desire, play gin rummy naked.

"When will men ever grow up?" flared-nostril women readers perhaps are saying.

Most of us never will, because of the Tree House Syndrome. When men are boys, they build tree houses, or other assorted edifices, in order to have a secret place to go with their friends where there aren't any girls to tell them how stupid they are, or how they should move the orange crate over near the cardboard box that serves as a table, in order to give the room more symmetry.

We need this getaway all our lives in order to gather our wits and share the goodness that is brotherhood.

And play gin rummy naked if we want to.

Men have given up so much of what was once their exclusive space as it is. And some of it we needed to share. Like boardrooms and mastheads and offices on the top floors.

But at this club, at least, men have drawn the line at golf.

"What I like most about this club," said a friend who was also a guest, "is there aren't even any ladies' tees. You can hit from all the way up front and not feel like a wimp."

Indeed.

Women in Running Shoes Brought to Heel

WASHINGTON—My ride was late, so as I waited on the sidewalk in downtown Washington, I people-watched.

I had seen the phenomenon I'm about to discuss in other large cities, but here in Washington there seem to be more instances of it. I'm speaking of the fact that when females in the workplace are out of their offices, many are now walking around in their otherwise attractive outfits in running shoes.

I am told that women wear these shoes to and from work and when they go to lunch, but once they are in their offices, they put on regular shoes, ones with heels that are more suited to the rest of their clothing.

I asked a female colleague about this once, and she explained, "We do it for comfort. You just can't imagine how doing a lot of walking in heels can absolutely kill your feet."

I can understand that. I've never personally done a lot of walking (or any walking, for that matter) in a pair of heels, but I can imagine how one's feet would feel afterward.

Still, I've got to say this:

Comfort or no comfort, wearing a pair of running shoes with a dress does to the attractiveness of a woman what a large tattoo does to a man.

It's downright displeasing to the eye. In a word—ugly.

And I hate to use the T-word, but I feel compelled.

It's Tacky.

At a gathering later in the evening I asked a Washington woman, who had had the good sense not to show up at a cocktail party wearing a pair of Reeboks, why this practice seemed so prevalent in Washington.

"I don't think it has anything to do with politics," she said. "Maybe Washington women just have to walk more than women in other cities. Why do you ask?"

Diplomacy has never been my strong suit. I looked at her square in her eyes and said, "Because it's tacky."

She threw a sausage ball at me and then huffed away in disgust.

But that didn't change my opinion. I don't think I have any sort of foot fetish, but women in sexy shoes have always caught my eye.

I recall the first time I saw Kathy Sue Loudermilk in a pair of high heels. It was at the annual Moreland Fourth of July barbecue. She was also wearing her tight pink sweater (the one they retired in the trophy case when she graduated from high school), a pair of short shoes, and eight-inch spike heels.

When the preacher, who was helping make the coleslaw, saw her, he said, "Lord, Thou dost make some lovely things."

I don't think he was talking about the cabbage he was putting in the coleslaw.

Said my boyhood friend and idol, Weyman C. Wannamaker,

Jr., a great American, when he saw Kathy Sue, "You put something besides them heels on that body, and you done put retreads on a Rolls-Royce."

And here I stand on a downtown sidewalk in our nation's capital, and eight out of ten women I see look like they went to the Sears tire store to shop for shoes.

The Lord does, indeed, make some lovely things, and I'm certain the Almighty had no intention they walk around in what amounts to glorified, overpriced, rubber-soled clodhoppers.

Your feet hurt, ladies? See Dr. Scholl.

Tacky. Tacky. Tacky.

I think I have made myself abundantly clear.

Women Wearing Ties

I saw a woman on an airplane the other day who was wearing a tie. I don't think I had ever seen a woman wearing a tie before.

I thought only men wore ties to make up for the fact we don't have to get pregnant.

The woman in the tie looked like one of those big-time business women who owns her own condo, a BMW and a fluffy cat.

"Excuse me," I said to the woman. "I was just wondering why you are wearing a tie."

"Why not?" the woman asked me back.

"Well," I said, "I thought only men wore ties."

"You obviously are one of those Neanderthal redneck men who think women have no place in your world," said the woman, who was very irritated by my comment.

"Not at all, madam," I interrupted. "I certainly believe if a woman can do the same job as a man, she deserves the opportunity to do so and she should get the same pay as a man.

"The only thing I'm against women doing is voting and driving," I went on, in jest, of course.

I forgot, however, that the feminist movement is totally devoid of a sense of humor. I should have known the woman wouldn't take my little barb in the frivolous spirit in which it was intended.

Her eyes bugged out, her face turned red and the veins in her neck popped out in anger. She called me several unprintable names, a couple of which I have never heard before, leading me to believe women not only have equaled men in the ability to curse, but may have exceeded us.

I thought the woman was going to have a stroke, so I suggested she loosen her tie. She did, and in a few minutes she seemed as calm as possible under the circumstances.

Upon some quiet reflection regarding this incident, I came to the conclusion that women certainly have a right to wear a tie anywhere at anytime.

In fact, I think it is only fair that all women be made to wear ties and men be allowed to stop the silly practice.

I quit wearing ties everywhere except to funerals of close friends several years ago when I decided I had had enough of being uncomfortable.

But I'm lucky. I don't have a real job like most men, so I can get away with not wearing a tie.

Ties are detrimental to men's health. Men who have to wear ties all the time tend to be high-strung and nervous because they've got this piece of cloth tied tightly around their necks. It's ties, not cholesterol, that cause most heart attacks and strokes.

Also, besides being terribly uncomfortable and unhealthy, it is a known fact that wearing a tie eventually leads to baldness. The tie hinders the circulation to the scalp and that's why men's hair falls out.

You don't see many bald-headed women, do you? Of course not. That's because they don't wear ties.

But it's high time they did. And it's high time men were relieved of this burden.

Imagine if the tie tables were turned and it was women who had to wear ties to get into a fancy restaurant. You walk in with your lady and she has forgotten her tie.

"You may enter, sir," the maître d' would say, "but Baldy there needs a tie."

What a simply delicious fantasy.

Women Drivers

During my recent recuperative period, I was not allowed to drive. Therefore, I had to elicit the help of others to drive me around to various appointments.

Once I even had a woman drive me.

I don't really have anything against women drivers, and statistics prove women actually are safer drivers than men.

However, there are certain facets of operating a motorized vehicle that women don't know beans about, and I seized the opportunity while having a woman drive me to attempt to teach at least one female person some of the finer points of motorized vehicling.

I must say this young woman was totally understanding about this learning experience.

"Why don't you just sit there and keep your mouth shut? I took driver's ed in high school," said my chauffeurette.

I knew, however, she was only kidding and was eager to learn, so I began with pulling up underneath an overhead signal light when waiting to turn left in traffic.

If a driver does not pull under a light when waiting to turn left in traffic and stays back behind the light, then the light will change back to red without anybody being able to turn left and motorists eventually will have to begin new lives for themselves in the line of traffic.

"Pull up all the way underneath the light and while it is changing back to red, you will be able to turn left," I coached my student.

"One more word out of you and you'll be back in the hospital," she said.

Next, we tackled parallel parking. Women cannot parallel park. They try, and, after failing, simply abandon their cars half in and half out of the parking space.

"The key here," I said, "is to pull up even with the car in front of the parking place and then *back* into it."

"Why don't you back into a deep hole?" suggested the lady.

I also discussed using the proper lane while driving on an expressway. The main point I wanted to make was the left lane was the passing lane and should not be used as the lane in which to cruise at eleven miles per hour.

Often I am driving on an expressway, and I end up behind a woman who is cruising in the left lane at eleven miles per hour. These are the times I wish I had machine guns underneath my headlights.

I also went into such things as not applying eye shadow or combing hair while driving, not backing up on the expressway to catch a missed exit, and not stopping on a busy street to discuss Thursday's doubles match with a friend who is driving the other way.

I mentioned dimming lights when meeting an oncoming vehicle at night, not searching through a pocketbook for gum while driving over thirty, not parking in fire lanes at shopping centers so as not to miss one minute of a shoe sale, and all the other things women do that are wrong when they drive.

When the lesson was over, I felt I had done at least something to promote better driving by our female friends.

"Women," I said to the taxi driver who took me home after I was put out on the street, helpless, "they don't appreciate anything."

"Zip it, creep, or I'll close that other eye," she said.

Accept Our Apologies, Mrs. President

What gets me about the women at Wellesley who said they were outraged by the choice of Barbara Bush as their commencement speaker is, Who do these little tarts think they are?

Barbara Bush is the first lady. Like Dolley Madison, a great American. Like Eleanor Roosevelt. Like Jackie, who was admired by the world.

Like Betty Ford, who proved to be one helluva tough lady. Like Rosalynn Carter, the original Steel Magnolia. Even like Nancy Reagan, who ran the country during her husband's naps.

Okay, so it was with the help of an astrologer, but let's not get bogged down with details here.

Barbara Bush sleeps with the president of the United States, and it is extremely difficult not to be influenced by one's bedmate.

After the day's discussions, meetings, and briefings, it comes down to George and Barbara: When they're alone under the sheets, we must know the president occasionally asks of his wife, "What in the devil am I going to do about the situation in Lithuania?"

And even if he doesn't ask, don't you think Barbara, just after the lights go off, says to her husband, the president, "I've been thinking, George, and here's what you ought to do about, etc."

Barbara Bush, in other words, is probably the most influential woman in the country right now.

So where do a bunch of twentyish college students get the high-handedness to say they are outraged because Mrs. President has been asked to speak to them?

So Barbara Bush has been a housewife and a mother and has gained recognition behind the achievements of her husband.

Didn't these women have mothers? How many of them stayed home to raise their children while the old man was out working his tail off to get the money to send them to a spiffy school?

Would they be outraged to hear their own mothers get up in front of their classmates and tell of their struggles they went through and the sacrifices they made to give their child a good home and an opportunity to educate herself rather than wind up a cocktail waitress?

To slap Barbara Bush in the face, as the Wellesley group most certainly did, was to slap a lot of other good and fine women and say to them, "You sold out by getting married and having kids and supporting your husband. You're not worthy of our respect."

I wonder where these children will be twenty years from now.

A lot of them will be successful professionally, I'm sure. Perhaps there are future CEOs in the crowd. Maybe even the first woman president.

But how many of them will also leave their top-floor office suites and go home to a cat?

How many of them will be forty and rich and powerful, but won't have married, won't have had children, because they thought it was a cop-out?

So they are high-and-mighty now, considering themselves above hearing the wife of the president of the United States offer them a little advice, even if some of it might have been motherly.

That's a shame. Not everything was bad about the roles women of Mrs. Bush's era played.

There needed to be changes and there have been, but Barbara Bush has seen things and heard things and experienced things that could have benefited the women of Wellesley, and they have acted like juveniles.

I hope they all get big thighs.

Advertising for Sex

We have before us the case of a young woman from Fort Lauderdale who went out with her girlfriend one evening dressed in a sea-green tank top and a ruffled miniskirt. Actually, it's what she did not have on that is the key issue here. She didn't have on any underpants.

She gets raped by a twenty-six-year-old man, and then a jury ups and acquits him because, in the words of the jury foreman, the victim "advertised for sex."

Obviously, there have been outcries of injustice, and how can I remain silent when so many others have seen the wrong here and have made public their disdain for the obviously Neander-thal thinking of the jury?

Here's the deal:

You see a woman out in public dressed in a sea-green tank top and a ruffled miniskirt and you say to yourself, "Hey, this chick probably isn't wearing any underwear, either, which obviously means she obviously wants to do the dirty deed."

Okay, so there's some basis for logic there, I suppose, but here's the spoiler, Big Boy.

Just because she's advertising for sex, it doesn't necessarily mean she's advertising for sex with you.

She could be advertising for sex with her boyfriend, Harold, who's meeting her later.

She could be advertising for sex with her husband. Just because you're married doesn't mean you can't still be kinky. She even could be advertising for sex with a movie producer who might be hanging out and happen to see her, and a month from now, she'll be co-starring with Mel Gibson.

Here's all the jury had to know:

Did this woman want to have sex with the creep who raped her? The answer is, of course, no.

But did the man force her to have sex with him?

The answer is, of course, yes.

Then it doesn't matter if she were walking around buck naked. To force someone into sex is rape, and it doesn't say anywhere that it doesn't count if the victim is provocatively dressed.

Send the creep to the Big House. If you don't, what happens the next time he sees a woman dressed in a sea-green tank top and a ruffled miniskirt?

If it was okay for him to rape the first one, why not number two?

Listen, I'm a man, and I know the stirrings that loose themselves when I see a woman dressed in something she obviously isn't wearing to a Junior League meeting.

But there are ways a man can soothe himself when visited upon by such stirrings. Think of the least sexy thing you can think of. Like Harry Truman. Or gallbladder surgery. Or the infield-fly rule. And, if none of that works, there's still the cold shower.

Just because you're wearing dancing shoes doesn't necessarily mean you want to dance. And just because a woman isn't wearing underwear doesn't necessarily mean she is there for the taking.

4 MEN

The Inside of My Tree House

Wilton Public Library
106 E. 4th, Box 447
52778

James E. Arrowood
Patron Number: 99002314
Date: 02/21/01   Time: 12:00

Materials being checked out:

108571 It wasn't always easy, but I sure
    Date due: 03/14/01

Materials currently checked out:

    NONE

Materials with fines:

    NONE

Hours: Mon & Wed -- Noon to 8 p.m.
Tues & Thurs -- Noon to 6 p.m.
Fri & Sat -- 10 am to 2 p.m.: Sun 2-6 pm
Phone: 732-2583
http://showcase.netins.net/web/wiltonpl

Mahvelous Memories

I lived with my father only six years, the first six years of my life, but I remember vividly so many of his characteristics, and I still find myself emulating many of them. The tie between many fathers and their sons is that enduring, I suppose. My mother taught me my ABCs. From my father, I learned the glories of going to the bathroom outside.

Perhaps this is just a Southern thing, but I have known many men who prefer relieving themselves out-of-doors rather than performing this bodily function in the impersonal setting of a modern-day toilet.

I can't explain this, but I, too, share the desire to go to the bathroom outdoors whenever it is convenient, and convenience usually depends on such things as weather conditions and the amount of privacy available.

I have a friend, a fellow Georgian, who learned outdoor pottying from his father.

"When I was in the first grade," he told me once, "the teacher asked me what I wanted to do when I grew up. I said that when I grew up I wanted to drink beer and pee outside like my daddy.

"The teacher sent a note home with me, asking for a counseling session with my father. When she told him what I said and chastised him a bit for putting such things in my head, Daddy said, 'My daddy peed outside, and his daddy before him. If my boy follows in my footsteps, he will be merely carrying on a great family tradition.' "

When Daddy came home from Korea, he could choose any post he wanted. Such comes from being an ex-prisoner of war. He chose Fort Benning, where he would become athletic officer and coach of the post baseball and basketball teams. We bought a new house in Columbus, Georgia, and there were woods in the back.

Before retiring each night, Daddy usually would announce he was going out for a breath of air. What he really did out there was go to the bathroom on one of the pine trees. If I happened to be up at the time—and usually I was, having become a night person early in life—I would accompany him.

"Will this hurt the trees, Daddy?" I asked.

"People peed on trees for thousands of years before we had toilets," he explained.

"Did cowboys pee on trees?" I wondered.

"Mostly on cactus," Daddy went on.

I developed quite a hero worship for Roy Rogers, King of the Cowboys, when I was five or six. One day, I was being Roy out in the backyard and it became necessary to go to the bathroom. Outlaws and Indians have to wait when a five-year-old Roy Rogers is called by nature.

I dismounted my broomstick, Trigger, and picked out an unassuming tree. As I was relieving myself, my mother came walking out to hang clothes on the line.

She spotted me and, with a horrified look on her face, asked, "What do you think you are doing, young man?" When my mother was happy, she called me by my name, or something like "sugar" or "sweetie." She always used "young man" in reference to me when she was angry.

"I'm peeing on a tree," I replied. I didn't see any good reason for denial, since she was only a few feet away from me and there I stood with my privates in my hand.

"And why are you doing that?" she demanded.

"Because we don't have any cactuses," I said, returning things to their proper place, zipping my pants back up, and riding away on Trigger to continue my involvement with the outlaws and Indians.

Mother didn't say anything else. She must have thought there was some logic to my explanation, but was too busy trying to figure out what on earth it could be to continue to berate my actions.

My grandfather also peed outside on occasion, and so did my uncles and male cousins. My childhood friends did the same thing. After Boy Scout meetings in Moreland, it was fun to go up in front of the Methodist Church and pee on the road that ran downhill. The idea was to see whose stream would stay on the road the longest.

Once I held out all day so that I would have a better chance in the peeing contest after a Boy Scout meeting. We all went to the front of the church, where it was very dark and absolute privacy was maintainable. We could all run behind the church and hide if anybody happened to come by.

It was no contest that evening. If my stream hadn't eventually run into the Atlanta and West Point railroad at the bottom of the hill, it might have even passed the Scout hut and almost made it up the hill to David Covin's house. I think that going to the bathroom outside gives a man a certain closeness to nature.

Some people spend a lot of money on camping equipment and spend weeks in the wilderness when they could save themselves a lot of trouble simply by occasionally going out in their backyards to pee. They would get the same benefits as they get from camping and wouldn't have to sleep on the ground or suffer from insect bites and pinestraw and grit in their eggs every morning.

Fathers are also important to sons in learning the ropes around public rest rooms. I have noticed that over the past several years they have begun to put lower urinals in public rest rooms for children and short people.

This was not always the case, however. Often, I went into public rest rooms with my daddy at such events as ball games and movies, and I could not reach the urinal, so he would pick me up and hold me high enough to finish my business. It was a big day in my life when Daddy took me into a rest room at a movie and I was able to hit the target without him holding me up. I simply took a step back and arched it over the side of the urinal. Daddy was very proud of me, and I was very proud of myself, so much so that when we sat back down in the movie with my mother, I said in a loud voice, "Mother! I can pee by myself!" That got a bigger laugh from the audience than Judy Canova was getting on the screen.

I learned to wear boxer shorts from my father. He wore army-issue boxer shorts. Under no circumstances did he wear jockey shorts, which is what my mother tried to get me to wear.

"I want shorts like Daddy's," I would complain when she tried to put me in jockey shorts. I wasn't even impressed when she bought me some Roy Rogers jockey shorts with pictures of Roy, Dale, Trigger and Bullet on them. I couldn't speak for the rest of the family, but I was certain Roy Rogers didn't wear jockey shorts, and I figure his picture on a pair of jockey shorts was just some clever adult ruse to trick a child into wearing unsuitable underwear.

I have carried my aversion to jockey shorts into adulthood. Jim Palmer might be sexy to women in those skimpy little undershorts he models, but I remain loyal to those comfortable—albeit baggy—undershorts that provide more room than jockey shorts and will never ride up when it gets hot. I doubt any studies have been done on such a thing, but I would wager that a great many crimes of passion have been committed because some guy's jockey shorts have ridden up on a hot day and caused him great discomfort and his fuse to be greatly shortened.

I remember how my daddy smelled after he shaved each morning. He smelled like Old Spice. I don't care what Pete Rose and Aqua Velva say, when a man wants to smell like a man, he wears Old Spice. I still keep a bottle of Old Spice in my bathroom. I admit I am mostly a Gray Flannel man, having been introduced to that fragrance by my third wife, whose daddy wore Gray Flannel, but I still pull out my Old Spice occasionally and rub a couple of splashes onto my face. It reminds me of Daddy.

His favorite food was fried salmon patties with hot biscuits and gravy. Mother cooked it at least once a week.

"Mahvelous salmon [he pronounced it as God intended and as the spelling insists, "sal-mon," not "sa-mon"] patties," he would roar across the table.

Occasionally I have convinced wives to prepare the same meal for me. And I will go to my grave insisting the correct pronunciation is "sal-mon."

Daddy drank more ice water than any man alive. We were driving once through a hot Georgia summer afternoon. He stopped for gas and asked the man if he had any ice water available. This is pre-OPEC, of course, when gasoline was eighteen cents a gallon and service stations still cleaned your windshield, checked your oil, and were friendly about it and occasionally even gave you plates and dishes for gasoline purchases.

The man at the service station came out with a cup of water. Daddy gulped it down and asked, please, for another. When it came time to pay his bill, the man said, "That's five dollars for the gas and a dime for the water." Daddy was stunned.

"You have charged me a dime for two sips of water?" he asked.

The man assured him that he had.

"In the name of God," Daddy said, "that's the same thing you get for a 'dope' [which is what he called any soft drink]."

"If you feel that way about it," the man said, "keep your damn dime."

"No," said Daddy, "if you're so hard up you've got to sell water, then I want you to have it. But I shall suggest in my prayers, it would be altogether fitting if your well ran dry. Good day."

The primary reason I have been able to avoid drinking Perrier is because I am certain my father would have considered paying $1.50 for a bottle of water outrageous.

Daddy's favorite actress was Joan Crawford. I was appalled at Mommie Dearest and I thought Faye Dunaway was atrocious in the title role of the movie.

Daddy, when he wasn't in uniform, wore bow ties. Bow ties are coming back, and, recently, I bought myself one. When I figure out how to tie it, I will wear it.

Daddy hated beets. So do I. Daddy loved George Patton. I

have seen the Patton movie at least a dozen times and have read two biographies.

Daddy snored. I used to practice snoring after I went to bed so I could be like Daddy. Now, I don't have to practice. He would be proud of my snoring.

Daddy was a Dodger fan. I still am.

Daddy went to the University of Georgia. So did I.

Daddy was a Methodist. So am I.

Daddy got fat after he got back from Korea. The Lord had led him to numerous heaping plates of fried chicken. I was a skinny kid all the way through high school and college. Afterwards, I began to put on weight. The more I gained, the more I looked like my daddy. It was only after he died that I did something about my weight. But he used to call himself "Chief Two-Belly," and that hint of a second paunch below my stomach is still there and will remain.

I got Daddy's skinny legs and big feet. I got his eyes, green, and his fair, freckled skin. I got his hair. Daddy would have never grown bald. My barber has assured me I won't either.

My daddy taught me to laugh. He sang me funny songs when I was a child.

My favorites were those with military themes, such as:

> *There's a soldier in the grass,*
> *With a bullet in his ass,*
> *Get it out, get it out*
> *Like a good Girl Scout.*

Then there was the marching cadence:

See that soldier,
Big and mean,
See that soldier,
Big and mean,
Somebody peed in his canteen,
Somebody peed in his canteen.
Go to your left, your right,
your left,
Go to your left, your right,
your left.

Unfortunately, one thing I didn't inherit from my father was his musical ability. I had a difficult time playing sticks in the third-grade rhythm band, and I can't sing a lick. But I can talk like Daddy did. As a matter of fact, I can talk exactly like he did. It is impossible to re-create that voice in print, but my impression of Daddy is impeccable. He had pet phrases. "Mahvelous," of course. When he was astounded by something, Daddy would say, "In the name of God!"

Instead of "every" he said "ev'ey," as in "Ev'eything is going to be all right."

He preferred the British pronunciation of certain words. He didn't say "cem-i-terry," he said "cem-i-tree." He didn't say "mil-i-terry." He said, "mil-i-tree." I had a stepbrother named Bob. When Daddy would speak to him, he would say, "Roh-but, Roh-but, Roh-but."

He referred to me as "Lewis Junior," and he would string out the "Junior" into "June-yuh." "Won-duh-ful" sometimes was substituted for "mahvelous."

"Great God!" was a substitute, I just remembered, for his astounded "In the name of God!"

He spoke loudly. He was one of those people who couldn't whisper even if he tried.

His voice commanded attention. He was never ignored in his life. When he spoke from a dais or a pulpit, his voice filled the room, the words catapulted from his mouth and caromed off the walls.

"Nobody can defeat the American soldier!" he would roar to his listeners. "The American army is the finest military machine the world has ever seen! And George Patton was right. We are going to have to fight the Rooshans [his word for Russians] sooner or later, and I don't know why we didn't do it while we were still over there!"

Later, after Daddy had died, I received a letter from one of his former students at a north Georgia mountain high school. Over the years I have been amazed to find out all the places he taught and worked. He could, in fact, talk his way into and out of almost any situation. The former student wrote, "One thing I always will remember about your daddy is he had morning devotion each day, and his prayers were just great! They were even funny, and he would always end them with '. . . And, Lord, please keep us safe from the Rooshans.'"

He had a number of Rooshan stories from the war. "When we got to Berlin in forty-five," he would begin, "I pulled detention duty. I had two or three hundred Rooshans in the compound for doing one thing or another.

"I never saw people like the Rooshans. They were the craziest bunch of people I ever ran into in my life. We had a high fence around the compound with barbed wire on top. They would stay in there until they saw somebody ride by on a bicycle outside. They were fascinated by bicycles. They'd just climb that fence like it wasn't there, chase down whoever was on the bicycle and knock him off. Then, they'd ride around on the bicycle for a little while and then put it down and climb back over the fence into the compound.

"And I'll tell you something, the Rooshan women were just as tough as the Rooshan men and just as ugly, too. The biggest problem we had with 'em was to convince them not to drink out of the toilets. They thought they were water fountains. And one day, we're going to have to fight 'em. Lord, I'd hate to have to fight some of those Rooshan women."

He drank buttermilk with every meal, and he was fond of his "Snellville midnight milkshake." I couldn't drink buttermilk as a child, and I still can't drink it. Not only is the taste horribly sour, but there is nothing that looks worse than a glass after it has had buttermilk in it.

"In the name of God, son," he would say to me when I turned up my nose at buttermilk, "there is nothing better in this world than a cold glass of buttermilk. I am convinced it will heal the sick and raise the dead."

Some of those memories are nearly forty years old, but they are indelible and they are a comfort.

To love someone unconditionally—as I loved Daddy—is to remember each detail of their personage, to remember isolated and long-past moments together, to remember nuances that made such an object of love unique and impossible to replace.

That is why I remember, and cherish, the memories of the man's hair, his smell, his likes and dislikes, his speech, and his idiosyncracies.

We had such a little time together. War took him away.

Then he came back for a short time before he was gone again. He never would return on a full-time basis.

Maybe that is why each of the nuances, each of the jokes and stories, each of the memories is so priceless to me. I have some pictures of my father. I have that packet of war records. I have the flag that was across his casket. I have his Bronze Star and his Purple Hearts in a frame and they hang on my wall.

But what I don't have anymore is him. There will be no new memories made. That is why I cling to those I have with such tenacity.

Of Pissants and Men

I had a coach in the early '60s who referred to us as "faggots," "queers," and "homos." But when he really got mad, he'd go to "pissants," which gave me the idea that a pissant was worse than a faggot, queer, or homo, and those were really bad things to be in the early '60s.

Or maybe pissants, as well as being miserable and worthless, also had homosexual tendencies, which is why Southern coaches hated them so much and equated them with a sixteen-year-old boy who couldn't learn to hit the cutoff man on a throw from the outfield.

Yes, white Southern males who grew up when I did constantly were having their manhood challenged, and if you were a pissant, it probably almost meant you were homosexual, so you might as well be dead.

And we've all grown up to be homophobic? How could we have not? It was ingrained in us from our earliest years that a homosexual was a sissy, walked and talked funny, couldn't tackle or block his sister, had no business in the Boy Scouts, much less the military, and his mother allowed him to run around the house wearing one of her petticoats.

The closest I ever came to being called a faggot, queer, or homo was when my mother told one of her friends she was still having to tie my shoes and I was already nine. My mother's friend had a son in my class, and she told him.

At recess, her son said, in a voice you could have heard in Hogansville, which was seventeen miles away, "Lewis's mother still ties his shoes!"

The other children on the playground snickered and pointed at me. Frankie Garfield walked over and punched me in the arm, which made Marcus's nose bleed.

I tried to explain it was simply a matter of having little or no manual dexterity, but my classmates weren't listening, and I knew what they were thinking.

". . . Yeah, and he probably runs around wearing his mother's petticoat."

So, I had to prove my manhood. First, I thought of picking a fight with Frankie Garfield. Frankie would kill me, of course, but at least my legacy would be one of bravery, which might overcome the stupidity of picking a fight with Godzilla.

But I was never much of one for pain, which I certainly would feel. Frankie was a strong believer in slow death.

A boy in my class named Bobby Hosmer ate a live earthworm on the playground one day to impress the girls, and became the first Southerner ever to eat any bait, which would eventually be known as "sushi." Maybe I could eat a live earthworm. I also thought better of that, too. Throwing up, which I most certainly would do, was also a sign of weakness.

What I finally decided to do was to invite my friends over to the Atlanta and West Point Railroad tracks early one morning and prove my manhood by sticking my tongue onto one of the cold rails. It was rumored that a boy once stuck his tongue on a cold rail and then couldn't get it off. A few minutes later, the Crescent, westbound for Montgomery and New Orleans, came by and ran over his tongue and cut it slap off.

I had cringed every time I thought of that story, which everybody knew, but what better way could I show my manhood than by risking my tongue to a speeding passenger train?

I took a group of five over to the tracks one cold Saturday morning.

"I am going to stick my tongue to one of these rails," I announced, "because I am not afraid I won't be able to get it off and a train will come by and cut it slap off."

I must admit, however, I knew the westbound Crescent wouldn't be highballing through town—the train didn't stop in Moreland anymore—until much later in the day, and the worst thing that could happen to me was my friends would have to pull me and my tongue off the rail and all I might lose was a little skin off the bottom.

So I got down on my hands and knees and stuck my tongue to one of the cold rails. What I hadn't thought of, however, was that the *east*bound Crescent on its way to Atlanta was due a few seconds after I put my tongue to the rail.

As my friends stood and watched in complete awe, I heard the blare of the front-end diesel horn, as it rounded the curve a half-mile down the road.

What if my tongue really was stuck to the rail? The train was getting closer now. Fortunately, I was able to determine my tongue wasn't stuck, and I could, in fact, get it out of the way of the train. But shouldn't I wait until the train was almost upon me before I pulled away from the tracks? I would be a hero. I would be a legend.

"Lewis waited till that train was bearing right down on him and his tongue, and at just the last second, he pulled his tongue off the rail and dived out of the way!" It would be in the county weekly newspaper. They might even give me a parade. *Grit* might even want a first-person story.

"The train's comin'! It's gonna cut Lewis's tongue off!" the girls screamed, and one even started crying and invoking the name of Jesus.

"Jesus Christ!" said my friend Dudley Stamps. "This ought to be somethin'!"

I waited until the Crescent was approximately 100 yards away and closing. Then I pulled my tongue off the rail and flipped myself backward away from the tracks. The Crescent's horn was sounding a constant warning signal. It roared by, and the engineer shook his fist.

But I had proved my manhood. I was not a homo, and I had witnesses to prove it. There was much talk about my boldness at school, and my mother found out about it and gave me a whipping. I also had a bad taste in my mouth for about a week due to the fact railroad tracks normally are quite filthy and have such substances as kerosene on them.

But the experience had been well worth it. I'd be dead if I had picked a fight with Frankie Garfield, and I'd rather drink a quart of kerosene than swallow an earthworm anytime.

The Test of a Wheel Man

When I was growing up, "peeling rubber" was referred to as "getting a wheel." For a boy-man driver of an automobile, it was another sign of weakness if he didn't "get a wheel" at every opportunity to do so.

Leaving school was a very important time to get a wheel. Only pissants, science-club members, and other social misfits didn't get a wheel when they left school. Most of them also usually were picked up by their mothers and driven home for their piano lessons.

Not so the cool, mature guys. When school was out at Newnan High (class of '64 here), it sounded like the Indy 500 time trials in the student parking lot. I'm convinced the cool, mature types single-handedly kept the Goodyear Tire Company in business between the years of 1960 and 1964, when I was in high school.

Getting a wheel involved putting your car in low gear, holding down the clutch, and revving on the engine for a good two or three minutes to build up momentum. Then you released the clutch and were doing sixty-five in a heartbeat. But that was only on your speedometer. Your tires were doing sixty-five, in one place. The result was that about half the tread on the tires your father bought you if you promised never to get a wheel was flying through the air. The resulting "errrrrrrrrk" sound they made on the concrete turned every head.

Once a car did lurch into forward motion, if you could get a wheel when you changed gears a second and third time, it meant you likely would end up on the cover of *Time* magazine as Man of the Year.

I received my driver's license at the LaGrange, Georgia, State Patrol headquarters on Saturday, October 20, 1962, my sixteenth birthday. The Newnan Georgia State Patrol office was a lot closer to Moreland, six miles, but that post didn't issue driver's licenses on the weekends.

Wait until Monday to get my driver's license when I'd been counting the days until this moment since they took the training wheels off my bike? No damn way.

My relationship with females began to go downhill the very first night I had my driver's license. I had a date with the woman who would later become my first wife, the lovely Paula. Naturally, our date was to go to the drive-in and do some major fogging up of the windows.

Our relationship, which ended in divorce in 1970, began to deteriorate when I decided that before we went to the drive-in, I'd cruise by the Dairy Queen, now that I finally had come of age to do such a wondrous thing.

The cruising part went well. Friends saw me behind the wheel of a car, which gave me status and acceptability. But when I started to pull out onto the highway for the drive-in, the trouble began.

A couple of my friends, who were sitting atop the hoods of their cars at the Dairy Queen because every mother in the country wouldn't allow their daughters to date them on account of their reputations as reckless drivers, screamed at me, "Hey, Lewis, get a wheel!"

As much as I had wanted to get my driver's license, I didn't do a lot of studying or thinking about automobiles beforehand. I didn't know one thing about carburetors, glass packs, Earl Scheib, painting flames on the side of your car, hanging foam-rubber dice over your rearview mirror, or putting your name on the driver's door and your girlfriend's name on the passenger door, which a lot of guys did, as in "Ducky" and "Sylvia."

And there was another problem. The automobile that I was driving had no clutch. It had an automatic transmission. It was a 1958 blue-and-white Pontiac. I actually preferred an automatic transmission, pissant as that might be, because a straight stick involved three foot pedals, instead of two, and a lot more mechanical knowledge and ability than I had at the time. (I'm still suffering from being mechanically impaired, as a matter of fact, manifested by the fact that I usually have to have an attendant come out to show me how to operate the pump when I pull into a self-serve filling station.)

So there I was, my moment to shine. To join that great fraternity of wheel-getters. To follow in the steps of some of the great wheel-getters and reckless drivers like Dudley Stamps and Raiford Smith, famed tire-tread destroyers, both.

I stopped before pulling out onto the highway, but I felt deep panic. I'd never gotten a wheel before. I knew it had something to do with stomping on the accelerator as hard as you could from an idling position.

But was I supposed to put the gear in "L" first or would "D" suffice?

I knew "D" was for "Drive." But what was this "L" thing?

I decided, in my panic, "L" probably stood for "Leap." So, I

pulled it down to "L," stomped the accelerator, and shot across
the street into a large trash receptacle in front of West's Body
Shop, which was located across the street from the Dairy
Queen.

My first thought was not, were my girlfriend and I dead, or
had I totaled the family '58 Pontiac. It was, did I get a wheel?

I was fairly certain I hadn't. One, I hadn't heard an
"errrrrrk." I had heard only a "huuuuuuuume!"—the sound a
'58 Pontiac makes when it is in low gear and somebody presses
the accelerator all the way to the floor and it lurches out from a
Dairy Queen and barely misses a collision with a produce truck
loaded with turnip greens and sweet potatoes and crashes into a
trash receptacle at West's Body Shop.

I then looked into the rearview mirror to see what the reaction had been to my first attempt to get a wheel. They were
doubled up with laughter. Some lay across car hoods on their
stomachs and beat on the hoods with their fists, howling and
bellowing.

I didn't get out of the car to check any damage. I had to leave
that place as quickly as possible. So I put my car in "R," backed
into the street, nearly colliding with the Greyhound bus from
Carrollton, turned it toward the drive-in and put the gear in "L"
again, and lead-footed the accelerator one more time. The Pontiac's rear end went toward the pavement, and the front shot
upward. But still no sound or smell of burning rubber. To make
matters worse, when we finally got to the drive-in, the movie
was Robert Mitchum in *Thunder Road*, where Robert Mitchum
played a guy who drove cars loaded with moonshine across
mountain roads. The movie lasted about an hour and a half. At
least three quarters of that were taken up by Robert Mitchum
getting wheels throughout the entire state of Tennessee.

My Daddies

I looked for my daddy, or parts of my daddy, in other men when I was a child, and I continued that practice on into adulthood. I never accepted anyone as Daddy's total replacement, but as I began to realize my own father never would play a full-time role in my life, I attempted to fill the voids he had left by seeking out men who reminded me of different portions of his personality.

There was a great man in Moreland when I was growing up. His name was Red Murphy. He was the postmaster in the tiny, white-framed Moreland post office on what we called "the square," which had a store and the post office and the knitting mill and the railroad tracks and an abandoned building that once had been a bank, on another side, and the Methodist church, all of which surrounded a vacant lot in the middle.

Mr. Red was a happy, red-faced man with a high-pitched voice. He had a pony and a wagon and on Sunday afternoons, he would ride around Moreland and take children on rides.

He also was one of the Boy Scout leaders. He taught me how to tie the knots it was necessary for me to learn to get my Tenderfoot ranking. You don't easily forget a man who played such a role in your development into a well-rounded individual.

Mr. Red, as the children called him, had three children. Mike was my age. Danny was older. Then there was a baby daughter, Molly. Mr. Red had a farm a half mile from my house, and down in those woods of his, Mike and I and our other friends partook of every pleasure available in the 1950s for rural children.

We dammed the creek a thousand times. We built a tree house and spent the night in it. We made cigarettes out of what we called "rabbit tobacco" and we rolled it with paper we tore out of the Sears Roebuck catalog. As long as you didn't inhale, smoking rabbit tobacco was at least a slightly pleasant experience.

We had rat killings. I have done many enjoyable things since I was a kid in Moreland, but few have held the excitement of a rat killing at Mr. Red Murphy's.

Mr. Red had a barn where he stored his corn. Rats like corn. I'm not certain exactly why, but rats like corn.

The best time to hold a rat killing is at night. The idea is to slip quietly into the barn where the corn is stored. Listen and you can hear the rats gnawing away at the corn.

This thing should have been on *Wide World of Sports* or something like that. It had to be more interesting than those people who are always diving off those cliffs in Mexico.

One person goes over to the light switch in the barn. When he hits the lights, it momentarily blinds the rats. In those precious few seconds the rats are blinded, they are sitting ducks— or rats—for .22 rifle fire.

Rat killing probably sounds a lot like the St. Valentine's Day Massacre. Blam! Blam! Blam! As fast as we could deliver them, the volleys poured in against the rats. It was no extraordinary event when we managed to send forty-five or fifty rats home to the Lord in one evening. The Murphys' grateful cats took care of most of the dead rats and the Murphys, unlike other local farmers, normally lost very little of their corn to the dreaded rodents.

Mr. Red had a heart attack and died when he was still a relatively young man. At the funeral, the preacher said, "Red's family has lost a wonderful, loving husband and father. Moreland has lost a great citizen. Moreland's children have lost their best friend."

I was fourteen when Mr. Red died. I remember looking at my friend Mike, Red's son, at the funeral. He looked stunned. There were no tears, just a blank stare.

I tried to imagine what it would be like if my daddy died. I couldn't imagine it. The thought was much too painful, too unthinkable.

I remembered that soon after Daddy came back from Korea, he and Mother talked about the fact he had a blood clot. I didn't know what that was, of course, but they seemed concerned and some of that anxiety naturally filtered down to me.

But my daddy had lived through Korea, I said to myself, and nothing could happen to him now. Children are much more able to comfort themselves with strained logic than are adults.

I did feel a loss when Mr. Red died. Mike and I used to walk home from grammar school together. I enjoyed telling him about my daddy, whom I always characterized as nothing less than a heroic superman. Mike always listened to me. He was a nice outlet.

"My daddy was a basketball player," I would say to Mike.

"Mine, too."

"Mine was the one who shot from outside."

"My daddy was a jumping center."

"Could your daddy shoot from outside?"

"I guess."

"My daddy never missed from the outside. Once, he scored fifty points in a game."

"Fifty?"

"Yeah," I would reply, knowing I had the conversation well in hand at that point. "And after he did that, he went out and showed all his soldiers how to fight a war."

If children had said such back then, I am certain Mike would have said, "Awesome."

I always have been drawn to strong men, whose courage and knowledge and abilities in manly practices could never be doubted. What I was doing was attempting to fill that unending sense of emptiness with which a son is left when there is no father to forge him security and contentment.

Bobby Entrekin's daddy knew more about sports than any other man in town. He was the one who explained the infield fly rule to me. He showed me how to choke up on a bat and how to run on my toes so my eyes wouldn't jiggle when I chased a fly ball.

Dudley Stamps's daddy ran a store. He smoked big cigars and let Dudley drive me around in the woods in his truck when we were years from a legal driver's license.

Eddie Estes's daddy built him a basketball goal, and one day when Eddie and I were playing, he showed us how to shoot hook shots.

Charlie Bohannon was scoutmaster. Once I got mad at something or other at a Scout meeting and ran home in tears. I went and hid in my bed. After the Scout meeting, Charlie came over to my house. I thought he was going to say something derogatory about me to Mother and H.B. I could hear him talking. All he talked about was what a good Scout I was and how he thought one day I would be an Eagle. When Charlie died, I remembered that incident. I wish I had thought of thanking him for not ratting on me.

Pete Moore organized a baseball team for boys in Moreland. He managed to get somebody to donate balls and bats. The second year we played, we even got uniforms.

He was a big man like Daddy. He had black, curly hair and he had hams for hands. Somebody said he used to be a catcher. We played our games against neighboring towns' teams behind the Moreland school building. When I pitched a no-hitter, he let me keep the game ball. When he talked to me during a game or during practice, he always put his arm around me.

I let him down only once. We were playing Arnco-Sargent from the other side of the county, and I was in center field. We led 6–5. Arnco-Sargent had runners at second and third and two out in the last inning.

The batter hit a looping fly ball toward me. I had momentarily lost interest in the game and was watching a teenage girl in tight shorts who was standing behind the visitors' bench when the ball was hit.

I got a late start and the ball got by me. Two runs were scored and we lost 7–6.

"Grizzard cost us the game," one of my teammates said to Mr. Pete when we came off the field. I was terribly embarrassed.

Mr. Pete put that arm around me and said, "Why don't you ride home with me and I'll get Sarah [his wife] to fix you some country steak and mashed potatoes?"

He never once mentioned my misplay. I ate country-fried steak and mashed potatoes until I was sick.

Bobby Norton, who later became a minister, was my seventh-grade basketball coach and homeroom teacher. He used to take me to Atlanta with him to see the Crackers play. He bought me vanilla custard ice cream at the ballpark like my daddy did.

There was this little girl in the seventh grade who was ugly and ran her mouth all the time. He was talking to some of the boys one day and somebody said something unflattering about this particular girl and Mr. Norton said, "Boys, you're going to be surprised because when she gets a little older, she's going to be a knockout and you'll all want her for a girlfriend."

I didn't believe him at the time, but he was absolutely right. I married her when she was nineteen.

Ronnie Jenkins's daddy, Mr. Bob, was a riot. He was the postmaster at Grantville, four miles down the road. When he retired, he entertained himself by entertaining Ronnie and me with wonderfully ribald stories from his youth.

We would sit out in the yard with him on hot days and he would call out to his wife, "Rachel, bring me another Ancient Age and Coke, and don't make this one so strong. Leave out some of that Coke."

It was Mr. Bob Jenkins who probably saved both his son's life and mine. When we were old enough to drive, we immediately turned to spending much of our spare time drinking beer. The normal procedure was to find a curb boy we could bribe into bringing a six-pack to our car.

"You boys been drinking beer?" Mr. Bob asked us one night when Ronnie and I arrived home. He was our friend. We admitted it.

"I tell you what I want you boys to do," he said. "When you want to drink some beer, I want you to bring it here to the house and drink it with me. That way you won't be out driving around in a car and I'll have somebody to talk to."

Danny Thompson's daddy took Danny and me to a square

dance once. We met these two girls and Danny's daddy let us take them out to his car and kiss on them until he was ready to leave the square dance. He was a kind man.

I often felt jealous of my friends, that they had fathers and that I had none. Even at a young age, I could sense how other children took their fathers for granted. I was too young to know to tell them of their great fortune.

At some time or other, I coveted most all my friends' fathers. I went to sleep at night with fantasies that by some strange miracle, I suddenly would be another boy, and I would still have the same mother, but that she would be married to this man or to that man who would be my real daddy, and I would know what it is like to have a daddy who never went away. It wasn't a mean fantasy. I didn't want anybody else to lose a father so that I could have one. I just wanted that feeling again, the one I felt the night I slept between both my parents, and I wanted it not for just one night or one week or even the year. I wanted it with no end to it. It seemed others had it that way. I just wanted my piece of the dream.

Such a desire, one whose strength probably is immeasurable, does not readily disappear.

A Hero's Passing

Daddy died August 12, 1970. He was fifty-six. I was twenty-three.

Aunt Dolly called me a week earlier to tell me Daddy was drinking again.

"He started drinking last week and wouldn't quit. I said, 'Major, I don't allow drinking in my house. My children just wouldn't stand for it.' "

"He said he didn't care about my children, that he was going to drink. I tried to take his bottle away from him, and he threatened me. I just don't know about anything like that, so I called the sheriff and he came and got him."

"Is he in jail?" I asked.

"I don't know," she said. "That was last night. I haven't heard anything from him since."

I called the sheriff's office.

"We just kept him overnight," I was told. "He got out this morning. I don't know where he went."

He went to Claxton. He started drinking again. He was walking down a street in Claxton when he collapsed.

Some people saw him fall. They called the police, who came

and tried to revive him. They said he had bruises on his head, as if someone had hit him.

The policeman took him to the hospital. How the hospital found me was from the letter I had written him. It was in his jacket pocket. He had no identification. He had no money.

A nurse called me in Atlanta and said a man had been admitted to the hospital carrying a letter that had my name and address on the envelope. I identified him as my father and asked what the matter with him was. She said he had a stroke and that he was in critical condition.

My wife and I had only recently separated. I was still in our house. I called Uncle John Wesley, Daddy's brother. He said he would ride with me to Claxton. It was a four-hour drive from Atlanta.

We got in at two in the morning. The night nurse let us into Daddy's room. She said he was in a semicoma, whatever that is. I saw the bruises on his face and head. I knew he was going to die.

Uncle John Wesley and I checked into a motel. I called Aunt Dolly in Pembroke to tell her where Daddy was.

"My daughter is driving in from California to take me away," she said.

"You're not coming to the hospital?" I asked her.

She said she wasn't.

I told her I thought Daddy was dying.

"My daughter told me not to go near the Major again," she said sadly.

I asked if she knew anything about the bruises on Daddy's head and face.

"I think he slipped in the tub," she said.

We stayed in Claxton with Daddy for four days. There was no change in his condition. He remained unconscious. The doctor said the stroke had been massive. I asked about the bruises.

"We think he probably got them when he fell from the stroke," the doctor said.

Uncle John Wesley said it looked like somebody had beaten him up.

"He probably got drunk and somebody rolled him for whatever money he had," was his explanation.

After the four days, we realized there was nothing more we could do at the hospital. Uncle John Wesley, then in his late sixties, needed to get back to work.

"I still mess with a few old used cars now and then," he said.

We drove back through a rainstorm. I had never been close to my uncle. I liked him, though. He always wore a big hat and smoked one Camel after another. His fingers were yellow from the several thousand miles of smoke that had passed over them.

He was a wise old man who lived into his eighties. He became the quintessential Grizzard to me. He was big, like all the Grizzards. He had his own brand of wit, dryer than my father's but perhaps more thoughtful.

"I never sold a car to a man who didn't deserve it," he said once.

On the way back to Atlanta he said what I had wanted to say. He said something that took away any guilt I had thinking death was the only hope Daddy had left. Uncle John Wesley said, "He don't deserve no more hell."

I kept in touch with the hospital after I returned home. Three days after I returned, the night nurse awakened me with a call. It was shortly after five in the morning.

"Your daddy's worse," she said.

"How bad is it?" I asked.

"You'd better come."

I drove Interstate 75 South toward Macon, ninety miles from Atlanta. The drive took me just over an hour. I left Macon on I-16 toward Savannah. The interstate ended near Soperton. I took the two-lane as fast as I dared on into Claxton. I made the 200-mile drive in just over three hours.

There were three men in the hospital room with Daddy when I arrived. They were friends from his church in Pembroke.

They stood at one end of his bed. Each had his hands folded in front of him. Country folk deal with death quietly. They do not fight it, generally. They are at peace with its inevitability. Their faith, forged in them for a lifetime, makes acceptance of death a ritual of calm and dignity.

"I'm Daddy's son," I said to them.

"Yes sir," one of the old men said. "The Major was always talking about you. He was very proud of you."

I was struck by their respectful stance toward me. All three men were much older than I, but their upbringing had taught them reverence for the family of the dying.

"Has the doctor been in?" I wanted to know.

"Came in just a while ago," one of the men said. "The Major has pneumonia."

He was blue. My daddy was blue. Each breath came with obvious labor.

"The doctor said he could go at any time," another of the men said.

So this was it. He would die in this bed, in this tiny hospital in this town with his son and three friends to watch him go.

I wanted to tell the three men his life story. I wanted them to know more of what they were seeing pass into the ages before them.

They knew only "the Major," a big, happy man with a thousand stories.

"Your daddy was a blessing to our community and church," one of them said.

Tell me about it, I thought. He sang and played for you, didn't he? And he made you laugh for a time and forget your troubles. He wasn't like other men you knew. His personality was so forceful. He brought life to wherever he happened to be.

But you don't know all the story, I wanted to say. You don't know how brave he was. You don't know how he led men into battle. You don't know how many nights he spent doubting there would be another for him. You don't know about the hell in Korea, about the years of loneliness and wandering. You don't know my mother and how much he loved her. You don't know about the torment that followed him. You don't know there must be some black secret that is dying with him.

You don't know how he was when I was a little boy. How I cried for him when we thought he was lost, how we cried for him when he came back to us.

You don't know what a terrible waste you are witnessing. This was a special man, a gifted man, a man for whom there could have been no limit to his accomplishments.

But look at him. Death should not be inglorious for such a man. Better had he died heroically, felled in battle.

A nurse came into the room and checked his pulse. He is just a body to her, I thought, an aging, sputtering machine that she is monitoring for its inevitable passage into obsolescence.

I looked out of the window. The morning was steaming. I remembered how much he had hated hot weather. I remembered all the ice water I saw him drink.

He would pour it into his mouth in great gulps, and then when he had taken the glass away from his mouth he would roar, "What a mahvelous glass of water!" I almost laughed at the remembrance.

I thought of that voice, that magnificent voice and the way he used it as a tool. No man could talk like my daddy could talk. He spoke in symphonic overtures, this man. I imagined him suddenly opening his eyes and booming, "In the name of God, son, what on earth is happening here!"

I had vowed not to cry. This was another test of my manhood, another in a series of tests I was constantly giving myself, for no other reason than to prove my manhood in Daddy's sight. To cry now would be a sign of my weakness. To cry now would be to disavow my adulthood. I stood there alone with my dying father. There was no mother to turn to and bury my face against for comfort. This was mine.

He continued to struggle for each breath. I thought each he took would be his last, but after a grueling pause, there would be another. The blue in his face was deepening.

The silence is deafening at a death watch. I wanted some great and furious words to say. But none came. The three men were also silent. They obviously felt to speak and interrupt my grief would have been terribly out of place.

The last breath came. We all saw it and heard it. There was a sense of relieved sigh to it. Or maybe there wasn't. Maybe that was my imagination.

Seconds passed. Then, a minute was gone. I put my daddy's hand in mine. I held it tightly. Another minute passed. I would not speak. I knew I would not speak. Someone else would have to signal the end.

"I believe your daddy has passed," one of the men said.

I closed my eyes and held his hand. One of the men slipped out of the room. He came back with the nurse.

She took Daddy's other hand and checked for a pulse. She looked up at me and found my eyes. She said nothing to me, but her eyes were the messenger.

"I'll get the doctor," she said.

I continued to hold Daddy's hand.

The doctor came in. He put a stethoscope to Daddy's chest and listened.

"He's gone," the doctor said to me. The nurse pulled the sheet over Daddy's head. I still held on to his hand.

The nurse and the doctor left the room. One of the men walked toward me and put his arm around me.

"If it would be all right with you," he said, "I think we should have a word of prayer."

I nodded yes. The man prayed. I didn't shut my eyes. I kept staring at the form under the sheet. When the prayer was over, the men said if there was anything they could do . . . I thanked them for coming. They left the room.

I stood over the body, with Daddy's hand still in mine. I was dazed. I thought of trumpets. I wanted trumpets, goddammit! I wanted the pealing of bells. I wanted something more than the silence.

The helplessness I felt became immense. This is it, I thought. It is over and it had been so quiet, so lacking of drama. He breathed and then he didn't breathe anymore, and the nurses came and the doctor came and they pulled a sheet over his head and a man had said a prayer. That had been it.

Death is a sneaking son-of-a-bitch. It makes not a sound.

Real Men Don't . . . Don't Do What?

The other day I read an article about a Conference on Men and Masculinity. I think it is a grand idea to hold such a thing.

Over the past couple of decades, a lot of men have had to ask themselves a lot of tough questions about masculinity, such as "Should I keep wearing boxer shorts or switch to bikini briefs?" and "Should I get some curtains for this place?"

Masculinity used to be a simple thing to define. If you had hair on your chest, a deep voice, and belonged to a club that excluded women, you were masculine, or, as was the phrase of the time, "a man's man."

But all that changed. The feminist movement came along, and suddenly women were saying they preferred Phil Donahue over Charles Bronson.

It was okay to be sensitive. It was okay to cry.

Dennis the Menace took down the sign on his tree house that read NO GIRLS ALLOWED and welcomed Margaret inside.

Men's fashion rules changed. It was okay to wear pink. Then

it was okay to wear an earring. Then it was okay for a man to wear his hair with a ponytail in the back.

But the new rules of masculinity, as I've mentioned before, confused a lot of men, especially men my age, those who don't have enough hair left to make a ponytail in the first place and who are hurtling toward prostate trouble.

We learned masculinity from our fathers, our scoutmasters, and our high school coaches—veterans of World War II, stand-up guys who were against long hair and drank their beer from a bottle.

Our heroes were John Wayne and Aldo Ray. If Phil Donahue had been in our school, we would have beaten him up on the playground.

But look at us now. We are trying to fit in. Do we stay with Old Spice or switch to something with a name like Dusk Musk?

Do we use mousse (something we used to hunt) on our hair? Should we order a glass of white wine or stick with Budweiser? Should we discuss football when we are bonding, or the crisis in funding for the arts?

I overheard a comment made by a male friend the other day that is quite telling.

He's mid-forties, and he said, "I'm just glad my father didn't live long enough to see me playing golf with my wife on Saturdays and getting my hair cut in a beauty parlor."

As for my personal beliefs concerning masculinity, I have become more tolerant in the past years.

I have at least two male friends who have ponytails. One also wears an earring. They are still my good friends. I never ask them over to watch a tape of *Sands of Iwo Jima*, but they are still good friends.

I get my own hair cut where it's coed. I allow the waiter to pour my beer in a glass. I have a male friend who has a cat. I've stopped questioning his masculinity.

I believe women deserve equal pay with men. I read articles by women sportswriters. I don't believe there was ever a woman raped who was asking for it.

But I still wear boxer shorts, and the first time Margaret said, "You really should get some curtains for this place," it would be the last time she saw the inside of my tree house.

I haven't come that far, baby.

5 LOVE

Azaleas in Bloom,
Lizards in Need,
and Marriages in
Two Days Flat

When I Danced on the Ceiling

Each time I visit Savannah, Georgia, I recall the spring of 1963, when I was there, a boy of sixteen, and the azaleas were in bloom.

I was a member of the Key Club at my high school. I don't recall exactly what being in the Key Club involved, but I was a member of it and felt accepted, and that makes growing up a lot easier.

They held a state Key Club Convention in Savannah that year, and I went. Some of us bought some beer and drank it in our hotel rooms.

We also went to one of the convention meetings out of curiosity, and a boy from Atlanta who wore thick glasses and pants that were too short gave a speech on the importance of being good representatives of our schools, communities, and parents while we were out of town.

I felt a little guilty about the beer, but the feeling soon passed.

Who else went to the state convention that year was our Key Club sweetheart. Every Key Club chapter had a sweetheart. I'm not sure why that was, either, but it made sense twenty-four years ago.

Our sweetheart had red hair and I was in love with her and our principal knew what he was doing when he made her stay in a different hotel than the boys in our group.

I had tried to get somewhere with our sweetheart before, but I always stammered and looked down at my feet a lot when I tried to talk to her.

Normally, I never said a lot of "uh"s and "ah"s and "you know"s in conversation, but when I tried to talk to our red-headed sweetheart I always sounded like a baseball player being interviewed on television.

"I, uh, ah, you know, I, you know, I, uh, you know . . ." I would begin, and by that time she and her red hair would be looking for somebody without an apparent speech impediment.

But there was that one glorious time in Savannah at the state Key Club Convention.

There was a dance contest, and you don't have to talk when you dance.

Members drew straws to see who would get to dance with our sweetheart in the contest.

I won.

There were maybe fifty couples entered in the contest.

The band played "Stay," by Maurice Williams and the Zodiacs.

My partner and I were one of four finalists. And then there was only one other couple to challenge us.

My feet were winged and I was rhythm and grace, elegance and style, and I didn't sweat nearly as much as I usually did when I danced.

We won the dance contest, and somebody took a picture of us kissing on the mouth while holding our trophies. I may have felt that good two other times.

There isn't very much more to this story. I continued to make a fool of myself when I tried to talk to our sweetheart later, and she married somebody else and so did I.

But I still have my trophy and I still smile gently when I think of her, the dance contest, and the spring of 1963 when I was here, a boy of sixteen, and the azaleas were in bloom.

P.S.: Our principal passed on several years ago, so I don't think I'm going to get in any trouble for telling the part about the beer.

Lizards Need Love Too

It's been more than twenty years, but I've never forgotten the pretty, blond girl who sat next to me in a class I had at the University of Georgia.

She wore lovely sweaters. The only days I didn't notice her lovely hair and her lovely eyes were the days she wore her lovely sweaters.

I wanted to speak to her, to ask her out. I wanted to take her to the Alps Road Drive-in Theater in my 1958 red and white Chevrolet.

"Lovely sweater you are wearing this evening, my dear," I would say, looking deeply into her lovely eyes, stroking her lovely hair.

She would grab me as her passion soared out of control and we would spend the entire double feature kissing squarely upon one another's mouth, which is about as far as passion was allowed to soar back then.

But I was shy. I never asked her out, not to the Alps Road Drive-in Theater, not even to the Varsity for a double steak sandwich with extra onions and pickles.

I tried my best to speak to her, but nothing would come out. I wanted to whisper to her in class, "Lovely sweater you're wearing today, my dear," but it always hung there in my throat causing me to cough on her.

I wrote love poems to her and sonnets and even a dirty limerick in a wild, lustful moment. But I never showed them to her. I figured if I did, she would call campus security.

I suppose the real reason I never made any sort of move on the girl of my boyish dreams, however, was that I was realistic.

I was no day at the beach when I was in college, if you know what I mean. The term for individuals such as me in those days was "lizard."

I had short hair and big ears. I wore glasses. I had a large pimple on my nose that struck when I was a sophomore in high school. It didn't go away until I had been married a year and my wife made me go to the doctor and have it surgically removed.

My pants always seemed to be too short when I was in college. That would have come in handy had there been campus floods, I suppose, but all it really managed to do was expose the fact I hadn't yet gotten the word white socks were out.

I never asked the pretty, blond girl who sat next to me out on a date because I was a lizard, and I knew it, and I figured she did, too.

But the point of all this: While I was in the hospital recently I received a get-well card from this very same girl, now a grown woman, of course.

She said some very sweet things in the card. She said she enjoyed reading what I write. She even said she remembered sitting next to me in class. I never thought she even knew I was alive.

I was happy to get the card even though it was twenty years too late. But I also felt a certain amount of remorse. Dang my hesitancy. Dang my timidity. Dang my big ears.

I won't allow it to go any further than the card, of course. She's probably married with kids—and, anyway, they tore down the Alps Road Drive-in Theater.

But let this be a lesson to the young and foolish. Give in to the mad rushes of love! Never hold back when you are filled with the magic of romance! If nothing else works, try a tube of Clearasil!

Lizards need love, too. Take it from one who has been there.

Just Call Me "MAODWMNSPCG14HGWS"

I was glancing through the paper the other day and I came across the personal ads in the classified section.

Ever read those ads? They're much more interesting than reading the soybean futures on the financial pages, and I lost interest in Dick Tracy years ago.

One ad read, "GWM wants to meet GWM for travel and intimate relationship. Must be nonsmoker."

After some thinking (I'm so brilliant on the Jumble word game, having gotten "UTIGRA"—guitar—in fifteen seconds), I figured what the capital letters in the ads stood for.

"GWM," of course, is a "gay white male," and I'm thinking here's this gay guy who wants to travel and become intimate with another gay guy and he's got to know the facts about AIDS, but what he's concerned about is breathing secondhand smoke from his lover's cigarette.

Another ad read, "SWF wants SWM who's into jazz, the classics, vintage wines and hiking."

"SWF" and "SWM," I figure, have to stand for "single white female" and "single white male."

"Straight" is possible, too, but let's not get overly immersed in detail, and just who does this SWF think she is kidding here?

Any single white female who has to resort to taking out an ad to find a boyfriend would take a SWM who's into yodeling, *Hustler* magazine, Ripple and robbing convenience stores.

Still another ad read: "SBM, handsome, athletic, financially secure, wants SBF, 20s, who will be his princess."

If I were a SBF (single black female) I would want to know how this narcissist got his money and if being his princess meant I'd have to get tied up or do anything involving live animals.

I don't think I'd ever put an ad in the personal section, but if I ever did resort to such a thing, I'm afraid I'd have a difficult time getting all I wanted to say about myself in a few capital letters.

I'm a "DWM," a divorced white male (okay, an oft-DWM). On top of that I'm a "MAODWM," a "middle-aged-oft-divorced-white-male," and I don't smoke, which makes me a "MAODWMNS."

I'd also like for prospective companions to know I'm a Protestant, a college graduate, a 14-handicap golfer, and I snore, which now has me up to being a "MAODWM-NSPCG14HGWS."

Naturally I'd also want to point out I'm a dog lover who brushes his teeth regularly, still has his hair, loves egg sandwiches, and often entertains friends by doing a simply marvelous impression of FDR declaring war on the Japanese in 1941.

Now, how are you going to get all that in a classified ad?

If my social life reaches the desperate point, I can always go after the "SWHW"s.

Single Waffle House waitresses. They're around twenty-four hours a day and make the best egg sandwiches in town.

I Do (Not Really)

My buddy Hudspeth met a girl. He met her in the elevator at the newspaper. She worked for the company that supplied our vending machines. He got on the elevator to go down for coffee, and she was on her way there, too. Hudspeth got a date with her. All those nights on the streets, and he meets a girl on an elevator at the newspaper.

She clipped the butterfly's wings. All of a sudden, my running mate had been taken away.

That had a lot to do with why I got married for the second time. I was struck down at the newspaper, too.

I was sitting at my desk in the sports department. Tons of kids came in all the time. The tour guide would say, "This is the newsroom. Those are typewriters. There are the editors. There are the reporters. . . ."

So I'm sitting at my desk one day, and I hear a female voice say, "And that is the executive sports editor, Mr. Grizzard." Only the voice didn't pronounce my name as I pronounced it. The voice said "*Griz*-erd," as in "lizard"; not "Griz-*zard*" as in "yard" and "lard."

I looked up. She was gorgeous. Maybe cute is a better description. She was short. She had those eyes. Big, wide eyes. She was smiling as she spoke to the kids on the tour. Great smile. Big and wide like her eyes.

Her accent was decidedly Southern. It had a peculiar lilt. Syrupy, but not *too* syrupy. It was a small-town accent. Small-town accents were disappearing in the South. Small-town people were moving to the cities, and suddenly everybody was sounding like Nelson Nowhere on the television news.

The girl disappeared down the steps with the kids toward the composing room.

I called the public-relations department, which handled the tours for the kids. I asked the name of the girl. It was Kay.

I gave it an hour or two, then walked down to the fourth floor to PR. Kay was sitting at her desk.

"I need to talk to you," I said to her.

She looked up with those eyes.

"I heard you giving the tour," I went on. "You blew my last name."

"But aren't you Mr. *Griz*-erd?" she asked.

"It's Gri-*zard*," I said. Then followed it with, "Want to have dinner with me tonight?"

"Sure," she replied.

We went to dinner. We went to her apartment afterward, and she took out her guitar and sang songs to me.

It was over after that. She was from the low country of South Carolina. That was the accent.

She'd gone to college, but it hadn't worked out. There was a boy, and they were going to get married, but that hadn't worked out, either. She thought about becoming a flight attendant. A family friend had a connection at the Atlanta papers, and that's how she had got the tour-guide job. She'd keep it until she could get on with an airline.

Six months later, on a warm April afternoon in 1973, I looked at Big Eyes and she looked at me, and I just got caught up enough in that tender moment to blurt out, "Why don't we get married?"

I didn't think I'd ever find anything to top her, even in Harrison's. She could sing, and she was good to hold and fine to have, so I said what I said, and she said, "Let's do it."

And then she asked, "When?"

And, tempestuous fool that I was, I said, "Why not as soon as possible?"

I called my stepbrother, Ludlow Porch, because I knew he wouldn't tell me I was crazy, and I needed somebody to take care of some details.

"Ludlow," I said, "I've decided to get married again."

"What are you?" he asked. "Crazy?"

"But this is different," I said. "We have a lot in common."

"Oh, does she like to drink and chase women in Harrison's, too?"

"No," I insisted. "We both enjoy the same kind of music, for instance."

"I like Waylon Jennings, too," Ludlow said, "but it's no reason for me to marry him."

When he finally decided I was sober and determined, he asked what he could do to help. I said, "I want to have the wedding at your house, because there's not room for me and her and the preacher in either of our apartments. I also need you to get your wife to arrange for a cake and do some decorating, and I need you to find me a preacher. But be careful. The preacher who married me and my first wife quit the pulpit and went into the used-car business six months later. I blame him for a lot of our problems."

"I'll do what I can," said Ludlow.

"And one other thing," I said. "I want to ride the train to Fort Lauderdale for our honeymoon. Trains are romantic."

"There is still a train that goes from Atlanta to Florida?" he asked.

"No. We'll have to drive to Savannah to catch it. It comes through about two in the morning."

"Let me see if I have this straight," Ludlow said. "You want to get married for the second time, even though you were a complete failure as a husband on your first attempt, and you want to do it as quickly as possible, which I assume is as soon as you can get a license and your blood tests.

"Then, you want my lovely wife to obtain a cake and decorate the house, and then you want me to find a man of the cloth who has no intentions of going into the used-car game, and then you want me to reserve you two tickets on a train that you'll have to drive four hours after the wedding to catch at two o'clock in the morning. Is all that correct?"

"It is."

"Call me in the morning," said Ludlow. "I'll get on it right away."

Two evenings later, I stood with my bride-to-be in Ludlow's house. He was my best man. His wife was maid of honor. Ludlow's six kids just sort of hung out and watched.

And the preacher. Do you remember crooked Indian agents in the old B Westerns? That's what this guy looked like. He'd sell a Comanche a used car with a bad transmission in a heartbeat. He started the wedding by opening a Bible and uttering, "Well, according to this . . ."

It was quite obvious the man, who was wearing a toupee that looked a lot like a dead cat had been glued to the top of his head, was very inexperienced.

"Where did you find this guy?" I whispered to Ludlow as the preacher fumbled through his Bible looking for some verse he'd forgotten to mark.

"Who do you want on two days' notice?" my stepbrother replied. "Billy Graham?"

The wedding cake was a little dry, but I did think the black crepe paper Ludlow's wife had hung from the ceiling was a nice touch. "Lincoln's funeral probably looked a lot like this," I said to Ludlow.

We arrived at the Amtrak station in Savannah an hour before time. An old black man was sleeping on one of the benches. The only other person inside was the guy behind the ticket window.

"Train's two hours late," he said to me before I could say anything to him. "Trouble out of New York."

"The train's two hours late," I said to my wife of five hours.

She had voiced some hesitancy to spending our honeymoon night—or early morning—on a train, but I mentioned a Clark Gable movie I'd seen once where he was on a train with some actress I can't remember and they seemed to enjoy it a lot. Besides, I also pointed out what an adventure riding the train would be. I think she muttered, "This is more adventure than I can stand," when I told her the train was two hours late, but I couldn't be sure because it was hard to hear her words over the snores of the old black man sleeping on the bench.

Then things got ugly.

I told the ticket agent my name and that my wife and I had a bedroom sleeper compartment booked to Fort Lauderdale.

He asked me our names.

I told him.

"Nope," he said. "Got no reservations for a sleeper under that name. You'll have to go coach."

I would have screamed, but the old black man seemed to be sleeping so peacefully, and I didn't want to alarm my wife any further.

Imagine us starting out in life in coach where people who coughed a lot and carried their belongings in paper sacks would be located, and there would be no way to lie down.

"There obviously is some sort of mistake," I said to the ticket agent. "I know these reservations were made, and I must advise you also that that woman standing over there and I were just married, and if you don't come up with bedroom accommodations for us, we are still going to get on the train and go up in coach and perform wild sexual acts on one another, which will get us arrested, I am sure, but it also will disrupt the entire train and be terrible public relations for Amtrak when the story hits the papers."

Noticing the ticket agent was a frail man, who wheezed and was probably one of the ten people in the world I could frighten with physical violence, I also said, "Not only that, but before I board the train, I am going to come behind this window and kick you and punch you and pull out what is left of your hair and call you and members of your family terrible names. Then I'm going to spread the word over this entire community that you are a bed-wetting, homosexual communist. Do you have that clear?"

The ticket agent began making telephone calls. A few minutes later, he called me back to the window.

"It's the best I can do, I swear," he said. "There isn't any bedroom space available, but I can get a roomette."

For those unfamiliar with railroad sleeping accommodations, a bedroom will sleep two. A roomette will sleep one. Barely. A roomette is sort of like your closet with an army cot in it. Two small dogs would have trouble carrying out the mating process in a roomette.

Then it hit me. Ludlow. He did this on purpose. He purposely didn't make us any train reservations because the man has a sick sense of humor and decided to play a very cruel practical joke on two crazy kids in love.

I took the roomette because I had no other choice, then I phoned Ludlow and awakened him and said, "This is really funny."

"What's funny?" he asked back as he emerged from his sleep.

"You not making us any train reservations," I said, my voice bristling with anger. "We've wound up with one roomette. One or both of us could get hurt trying to carry out a honeymoon-night function in that small a space."

"You think *that's* funny?" said Ludlow. "Let me tell you what else is funny. Remember the guy with the weird toupee who married you?"

"How could I ever forget him?" I said.

"He was no preacher. He runs the Texaco down the street. I got him to marry you in case you changed your mind about all this during the honeymoon and needed an out."

I never mentioned that part to my new wife, of course. I was so convinced only death would do us apart, I felt Ludlow's idea of doing me what he considered a favor was anything of the kind. We were married now, and there would be no turning back.

You *can* have sex in a roomette on a train hurtling through the Florida night, by the way, but I didn't have the nerve to tell the chiropractor how I actually injured my back.

6 SEX

The Urges That Hit You While Hanging Sheetrock

Garden Tractors, Dictionaries, and Geography

I won't bore you with any intimate details of my early sex life, such as it was. Those first-time stories are generally overdone, and who wants to hear them in the first place?

What I will say, however, is that sex was on my mind a great deal when I was a child, and don't think if you have children they aren't the same. In fact, they probably think about sex even more than I did because I didn't have cable television, commercials discussing "maxi-pads," and music videos that could stir up youthful hormones in five states.

About all I had was the Sears Roebuck catalog, the dictionary, the occasional sex novel someone had pilfered from his father's sock drawer, and the *National Geographic*.

As soon as the new Sears Roebuck catalog came, my grandfather and I would sit down and look at the pictures of shotguns and garden tractors.

As soon as he tired of looking at shotguns and garden tractors, I would promptly return to the scuppernong vines—my personal den of iniquity—and turn to the ladies' underwear section.

Most of the women who posed for the catalog, by modern standards, were ugly and a bit overweight. But I had my imagination. Later, I would have the opportunity to go into bars where young ladies danced in the absolute and glorious nude, but there is truth to the idea that sexiness is best accomplished with a tease.

I also used the dictionary in order to pique my sexual interest by looking up dirty words, or words I thought at the time were dirty. You didn't see these words in print in newspapers or textbooks back then. These were mostly anatomical terms I would spring on my friends who either didn't have a dictionary at their homes or were not as sexually aware as myself and hadn't thought to look these words up.

After all those efforts to look up dirty words in practically every dictionary I came across, I never did strike gold. I never found the "F" word, *the* dirty word of all dirty words. Unabridged, my fanny.

But my efforts did lead me to the knowledge of a great many words I never would have been able to add to my vocabulary. Here are some examples:

1. *Fucoid:* of or like seaweed
2. *Fugger:* German family of merchants and bankers of the fifteenth to nineteenth centuries
3. *Fug:* the heavy air in a closed room, regarded as either oppressive and murky or warm and cozy
4. *Fukien:* province of southeast China on Taiwan Strait

One night over dinner, when I was about twelve, and had spent a good portion of the afternoon looking for dirty words in my dictionary, I said:

"Well, I guess everybody heard about the Fuggers eating all

that fucoid, and how they had to endure all the fug on their way to Fukien."

My grandmother fainted, and my mother took away my dictionary rights for a year.

The *National Geographic*, of course, has been used for years as a means for young people to get a clean shot at the human anatomy, thanks to the hundreds of pictorials *NG* has done regarding the lifestyle of still-primitive cultures in general, those where the women go around with no tops on in particular.

In my school, however, the librarian noticed how quickly the sections of the *Geographic* that featured the topless native women became frayed and dog-eared.

After that, when the new magazines arrived at school each month, she would go through *NG* with a pair of scissors and cut out all the good stuff and leave in the sections with close-up photographs of hummingbirds and one-cellular sea life. I lost all interest in geography after that. It seemed pointless.

Marching in the Rubber Band

The last thing I remember about condoms before, say, a couple of years ago, was the time Alvin Bates, the class nerd, brought one to chemistry class as part of a project to explain expanding gases.

Alvin got up in front of the class, not to mention Mr. Scoggins, the teacher, and dropped a couple of Alka-Seltzers into a shot glass. He then put a condom over the shot glass and whatever it is that bubbles out of Alka-Seltzer made the condom stick straight up.

The boys in the class laughed. The girls, with the exception of Adella Lemaster, who was very religious and ran screaming out of the class, all giggled. Mr. Scoggins cleared his throat several times and quickly told Alvin to cease his demonstration and sit down.

As it turned out, Alvin had no idea what he had done. As he was going through his father's sock drawer one day, looking for a black, over-the-calf pair to wear with his sandals and Bermuda shorts to a Sunday school picnic, Alvin came upon several coin-sized packages.

Always the inquisitive type and always eager for knowledge (Alvin subscribed to *Grit*, *Boys Life*, and *Popular Science*, and never missed *Mr. Wizard* on television), he opened one of the packages and discovered a curious balloonlike instrument.

He asked his father, who was the county agent for the Farm and Home Extension Service, to identify what he had found in the sock drawer.

Alvin's dad, Mr. Bates, told him it was a sheath used to keep carrots from getting hurt from sudden frosts. As Alvin planned his chemistry demonstration, he thought those carrot covers would be just the thing for his expanding-gases trick and took one from his dad's sock drawer.

I don't mention Alvin in the chapter regarding people who've never had sex, because I'm just not certain in his case. After college at Clemson, Alvin joined the Peace Corps and last I heard of him, he had been taken prisoner by some left-wing group attempting a coup in one of those countries that looks like an eye test when you spell it out.

Alvin was busy on a project to convince the natives to stop wearing loincloths and wear knee-length woolen shorts that had been donated by postal workers instead, when he was taken away by rebels.

In a terse statement in late 1969, the State Department denied there ever being an Alvin Bates in the Peace Corps.

Even if the rebels didn't execute him and released him back to the natives, I figure they probably hung him, or worse, for convincing them to take off their comfortable loincloths for those scratchy woolen shorts.

In either case, it's doubtful Alvin ever did know the particular joy of sex, but one can never be too sure when loincloths are involved. If I hear from Alvin and can clear this matter up before I finish this book, I will pass on any answer I might get for our question.

Anyway, after Alvin used the condom in chemistry class, I didn't hear much about condoms anymore until recently, when the AIDS scare came along.

That's because condoms (a.k.a. prophylactics, a.k.a. rubbers—and those are the only other names I ever knew them by) were virtually replaced by other means of birth control such as the Pill, contraceptive foam, and the IUD, which, incidentally, is DUI spelled backwards.

We must also remember that every condom machine in every truck stop displayed the notice "This product should be used for the prevention of disease only."

This, I presume, was so that if anybody used a condom and it leaked and somebody got pregnant anyway, they couldn't sue the condom company. There's no telling how much some lawyer charged condom companies for thinking of that.

There was, of course, a concern for getting venereal disease back then. Went the wisdom of the day, "Better not catch the clap because you're going to have a helluva time convincing your wife she's got to have a shot for *your* kidney infection."

But I remain certain that not one in a thousand condoms were used because of a fear of getting a disease. They were used because it was hell to pay if you got a girl pregnant in those days.

The girl's mother would send her off to a home and, if you lived in a small town, they'd talk about you for eons and the preacher would include you in his annual anti-fornication sermon, which, at home, always came just before the Fourth of July Street Dance, when the tempting moan of the steel guitar, mixed with the warm night air and six bottles of Calgary Malt Liquor, could fling a craving for the flesh on the saved and unsaved alike.

Having said that, however, let me also say there were only a couple of girls I knew of who got pregnant out of wedlock when I lived back home, and we're talking eighteen years here, which is to say either there was a lot of condom use going on or there wasn't much serious woo being pitched.

Quite frankly, I go for the latter explanation. As I have said, the sexual revolution was a ways off then, and in the immortal words of my boyhood friend and idol, Weyman C. Wannamaker, Jr., a great American, after thirty-four successive dates that didn't come across, "If I ever scored in this town, I'd take out an ad and announce it in the county paper."

Still, once we reached our teens, we felt to walk around without a condom in our wallets would be to ignore completely all the advantages of preparedness. God, what if lightning struck and there you were without, as we said back then, *protection*? (Later, this term became a byword of a number of feminine hygiene products' advertising campaigns, but let's don't get into that.)

There were a number of ways to come into possession of your first condom. You could take the easy route by finding out where your father kept his, or you could show your manhood by actually buying one for yourself.

There were even two ways of doing that. The easiest way was to go to a service station or truck stop and go into the men's room where the condom machines were located.

And what wondrous machines those were! Usually, there were several selections of condoms, as there are several selections in a gum or cigarette machine, not to mention other sexually related products, such as a cream called "Dee-Lay" to avoid premature getting through, and a tiny book of sex jokes everybody had already heard.

As far as their condoms were concerned, there was one that came in "exciting, exotic colors," another that featured a "nipple end," and then there was the celebrated "French Tickler," to be purchased at risk because of its ability to "drive her wild!"

There were certain procedures to follow when purchasing one's first condom in a rest room. First, you had to remember to bring quarters. To go to the cashier and ask for change and then to go directly into the rest room certainly would expose your intent.

Not only would that be embarrassing, but it also could get back to your mother.

The other thing to remember was, once you were safely inside the rest room, to lock the door. Then, it was absolutely necessary to slide the coin holder into the machine very quietly so nobody outside could hear and, again, know of your evil scheme.

There also was a time element involved here. One had to be mindful of just how long the exercise of buying a condom took. You had to stay in the bathroom long enough to, well, go to the bathroom, because if you came out quickly everybody would know. "Look at that kid," they'd say. "He didn't stay in the bathroom very long, so we know he was in there buying rubbers."

Of course, if you took too long, then there must have been something else you were doing in the bathroom other than using the facility, and what else could that be other than you were buying condoms?

The ultimate in obtaining a condom was, however, actually going into a drugstore and buying one across the counter from a pharmacist.

This took some guts, even if you lived in a large town and went to a drugstore where there was absolutely no chance of anybody you knew seeing you in this act.

Lee Marvin would have had a difficult time convincing *The Dirty Dozen* to attempt to pull off such a thing in a small town, however, where anybody from your Aunt Hattie to your typing teacher could catch you.

To be quite frank, I never got up the courage to buy a condom in a drugstore until I was in my middle thirties. I'm not certain why, but buying condoms in public always seemed to be letting a lot of other people in on the fact that you were having sex with somebody. You know the pharmacist is grinning inside, and will talk about you when you leave.

The other bad thing that could happen in this scenario is the machine could be broken or out of condoms and you would not only be denied the object of all your effort, but you'd lose your quarter, too.

You couldn't bang on the machine like you would a soft-drink box that took your money, because that would make a lot of noise. You couldn't go complain to the owner, either, because he would say something like "Son, you're too young to be buying something like that."

In fact, I learned later in life that some service-station and truck-stop owners had condom machines installed in their rest rooms but never had them filled.

"We even had one in the ladies' rest room where I worked," a man told me. "There never was anything in them, though, because no woman was going to complain that the rubber machine was out at a truck stop. No telling how much money the guy I worked for made with that scam."

Some guys had enough guts and bravura to pull it off when I was a kid though, and they were admired and spoken of in hushed, reverent tones.

Legend even had it that one twelve-year-old walked up to the pharmacist in Leebold's Drug Store and said, "I want a condom."

The pharmacist replied, "Son, are you sure that's what you want?"

"Yes sir," said the kid. "I want one of those French Ticklers, too."

"But don't you know what that will do to a woman, young man?" the pharmacist continued.

"No," said the kid, "but it'll make a goat jump six inches off the ground."

I know one more like that.

A young man meets a girl. They have a few dates, and at the young man's pleading, the girl agrees to have sex with him the following Saturday night at the drive-in theater. This is a modern-day story.

She insists, however, he bring protection—*that word again—so he goes down to the drugstore and walks back to the pharmacist and says, "I'll have a condom."*

The pharmacist winks and says, "Hot date, huh?"

"Can't miss," says the young man. "This girl is the hottest."

He walks to the door at the girl's home the following Saturday and she says, "Come in for a minute and meet my parents."

The young man meets the parents and then says to his date, "Honey, we can go to the drive-in anytime. Why don't we stay here and play Monopoly with your parents?"

The girl is quite befuddled, but the young man is insistent.

Around midnight, the young man yawns and indicates he must leave. The girl follows him to his car. She is angry.

"I didn't know," she says, "that you were such a fan of Monopoly."

"And I didn't know," he replies, "that your father was a pharmacist."

Fornication-Free

There are a lot of people who have never had sex. That's a stupid statement. Of course, there are. What I mean here is there are a lot of people we presume have had sex, but, it is my belief, they never have. We ought to get these people out of the way before we go any further.

I figure Richard Nixon has never had sex. I know he has children, but I think they were adopted, or fathered by Pat Boone as a favor, as I simply cannot picture Richard Nixon having sex.

For one thing, I'm convinced he was born in a dull, blue suit and has slept in one the rest of his life. I suppose you can sleep in a suit and still have sex, but I don't think Richard Nixon would even try it because he might get something on his tie, and Nixon strikes me as somebody who would absolutely hate to get something on his tie.

You've met people like that before. They're stuffy and fastidious and wear wing-tip shoes and you'd like to see them try to eat barbecued chicken without getting one speck of sauce somewhere on their persons.

Not only can I not picture Richard Nixon having sex, I can't picture anybody having sex with him, not even his wife, Pat, who probably feigned enough headaches during her married life that she could be the Advil poster child.

In order to have sex, you've got to have at least a little something cool or suave about you, and you've got to let your hair (as well as your pants) down at least a little.

I can't picture Nixon doing that. He might have sex if he could do it by mail, but that's about it.

The only reason we might believe that Nixon ever had sex is that when he said, "You won't have Dick Nixon to kick around anymore," he might have meant his S&M thing was in the past.

But I doubt Nixon was ever into whips and chains, except for the time G. Gordon Liddy came over to the Oval Office and asked Nixon to beat him up with a rubber hose so he could show the president his loyalty.

"Go fry yourself a rat, Gordon," the president probably said. "When I need some dirty work done, you'll be the first one I call."

That brings up Henry Kissinger, Nixon's secretary of state. I know that Henry was once hailed as Washington's most eligible bachelor before he married what's-her-name who's so thin and tall and thumps cigarette ashes on the floor of the White House at cocktail receptions (I was at a White House dinner once and saw her do it),* but I can't picture Henry Kissinger having sex, either.

And even if he did, I bet he never took off his glasses, and then spent thirty minutes analyzing the entire procedure and came to the ultimate conclusion, "Ve dum de doom ve dum de doom," which is how Henry Kissinger says, "This is a lot more

---

*Do it, as in thump ashes—not "do it."

fun than talking to the president about how he always wanted to be a sportswriter."

I don't think evangelist Jerry Falwell ever has had sex before, either, which some may feel difficult to believe what with the history of evangelism and its recent episodes of fooling around in the wrong pew. (See Bakker, Jim.)

I can see Elmer Gantry doing it every chance he got. In fact, I did see the movie *Elmer Gantry*, and I thought Burt Lancaster did a splendid job of portraying the Brother Gantry who had the hell hots for everything that wore a skirt and didn't sing bass. But not Jerry Falwell.

He looks too much like a frog to have had sex. The next time you see Jerry Falwell, notice how toadlike he looks. He looks like he could fling out his tongue and pick off an unassuming fly at twenty feet. He probably sits in his office and does that at night after counting his money.

Jerry Falwell seems to be the kind of person who, if he could, would get rid of sex forever. When he talks about sex, he uses the term "fornicating."

The only people who say "fornicating" are people who spit on you when they talk and started branding people with scarlet letters when witch-hunts went out of style.

The next time you hear Jerry Falwell talking about the evils of sex, watch how his eyes get wild and his lower lip trembles when he spits out the word "fornicate!"—which he always says with an exclamation point on the end. Examples:

"Jim Bakker *fornicated*!"

"They are *fornicating* on the campuses of this country!"

"The *fornicators* are in control of the media!"

"Kill the *fornicators*!"

Even back in biology class in 1962 when the teacher discussed the reproduction of the salamander (they weren't allowed to go any further than that), he didn't use the term "fornicate." He stuck to "fertilizes" and "mates with." Later, the biology teacher was caught fertilizing one of the substitute teachers over behind where he kept dead salamanders in jars of formaldehyde. He was kicked out of the school system and last we heard was out west somewhere trying to figure out just how turtles do it with that shell and all.

There was a rumor Jerry Falwell had once engaged in oral sex. That turned out not to be the case, however. All he did was stand in one corner of the room and trade "fornicate-you"s with Jim Bakker when they were trying to decide who was in charge of the PTL Club.

Here are some other people who I'm not sure ever have had sex and the reasons why:

PORTER WAGONER: By the time he gets all those rhinestones off, the feeling has passed.

XAVIERA HOLLANDER: All that's probably just a lot of talk.

DR. RUTH: Ditto, plus she's too short.

YASSIR ARAFAT: Too ugly.

WILBUR ON *MR. ED:* Ed had too much pride.

BROOKE SHIELDS: Her mother hasn't told her about it yet.

MARCEL MARCEAU:

DORIS DAY: Actually, she had sex before, but she gave it up when she became a virgin. (With apologies to Oscar Levant, who once said, "I knew Doris Day before she became a virgin.")

CONAN THE BARBARIAN: He wanted to have sex, but his shield and sword kept getting in the way.

PRINCE CHARLES: Much too proper to deal with anything so common. Sent in his sperm to Princess Di from his polo matches by Royal Courier.

BOY GEORGE: Neither sex will have him.

ROY ROGERS: The King of the Cowboys, my childhood hero, didn't have time for such frivolity what with things so rough out on the range, which also could mean Dale and Smiley Burnette were more than just friends.

HERSCHEL WALKER: Has always been shy around girls and there aren't any fast enough to catch him.

NAPOLEON BONAPARTE: Ever notice in his pictures his pants didn't have a fly?

WALLY AND THE BEAV: America wouldn't have stood for it.

MATT DILLON: God knows he had his chances after Miss Kitty closed the Longbranch, but that's the sort of stand-up, no-nonsense guy he was. The jury is still out on Festus, however.

ANDY GRIFFITH AND HELEN CRUMP: Want to go over to Mt. Pilot and eat Chinese?

SUPERMAN: Little-known fact he was impotent. That's what X-ray eyes will do for you.

IVAN THE TERRIBLE: Actually he had sex once. That's how he got his nickname.

GUNTHUR TOODY: If you have any idea whatsoever who Gunthur Toody was, you'll understand why he never had sex.

SANDRA DEE: Became pregnant in A *Summer Place* not from actually having sex, but from French kissing while lying down with Troy Donahue, which was known to cause pregnancies before 1964.

COLONEL SANDERS: Too busy chasing chickens around with an ax in his hand.

HELEN OF TROY: Helen Ripplemeyer, old-maid country store owner in Troy, Alabama, that is:

One day, a traveling salesman came into her store. He had been stung on the end of his business by a yellow jacket and it had swollen to three times its original size.

He unveiled his painful privates to Helen Ripplemeyer and said, "What can you give me for this?"

Without a moment's hesitation, Miss Ripplemeyer replied, "How about a '48 Packard, the store and three acres of land?"

The traveling salesman left in a panic and Helen was never the same afterwards, spending her time with her cats and lusting privately for television wrestlers.

Asexual Advice

The problem many men have is they get sexual urges, and the primary physical manifestation of the urges, at the worst possible time, such as while traveling on a public transport, while sitting around the pool, or while hanging Sheetrock, for that matter.

This, of course, can be terribly embarrassing.

The key, when a man finds himself in such a situation, is to turn his mind toward matters that are totally asexual.

I've used Harry Truman a great deal. There is absolutely no way to continue to be sexually aroused when one is thinking of Harry Truman.

Think about that big hat he wore, about the Truman Doctrine, or about his rather plain, piano-playing daughter, Margaret.

If you find yourself still somewhat aroused after thinking about Harry Truman, try Herbert Hoover or even Millard Fillmore. That ought to do it.

This also can be helpful while in the midst of sex. One of the most difficult tasks a man has during sex is, no matter how much he tries, he often cannot avoid finishing before his partner, thus embarrassing himself and disappointing his partner.

When a man feels his passion getting out of control, he can use Give 'Em Hell Harry or any of these asexual subjects:

INDIANA: I can't think of anything that is sexy about the state of Indiana.

ENGLISH PEAS: I detest English peas. Anybody who can obtain a sexual climax while thinking of English peas is a sick person.

THE ATLANTA BRAVES: This team is to baseball what Marjorie Main was to sex.

YOUR NEXT VISIT TO YOUR MOTHER-IN-LAW'S: Unless your mother-in-law still does a stage act involving poodles.

THE MORMON TABERNACLE CHOIR: If it weren't for having their own choir, Mormons would have even more babies.

THE SOPWITH CAMEL: But not the Fokker.

BETTY ANN COBBLEHAMMER: A girl in my school who had a flat nose, thick glasses, stringy hair, wore Dee Cee overalls and started dipping snuff when she was eleven.
Just think of snuff, for that matter.

HEMORRHOID MEDICINE COMMERCIALS: "Be sure to use only as directed." What do they think I'm going to do with that stuff, put it on a saltine cracker and eat it? Not me. I don't want to shrink up and be a little guy with little arms and legs.

YOUR NEXT VISIT TO YOUR DENTIST: On second thought, don't think of that. The first dirty movie I ever saw was in a friend's trailer in college. For a buck, he showed *Tillie Goes to the Dentist for a Filling and a Drilling.*

"Fooling Around" with Health Care

I totally agree we need to do something about the health-care crisis in this country. Anybody with my medical history knows not being able to get the proper doctoring can even be fatal.

But I, like others, wonder how we're going to pay for the new Bill and Hillary Health Package. I may have a solution.

You probably have already heard about using a possible "sin tax" to help defray the costs. Specifically that idea is to add another tax on cigarettes and possibly hard liquor. But why limit the tax to the sin of smoking? And smoking most certainly is a sin because it is pleasurable, and a lot of people frown on it.

Practically every sin has the same characteristics.

I suggest we also enact a sex tax to help pay for the new health program. Or, more specifically, a "fooling-around" sex tax. You wouldn't be taxed on sex that is not particularly pleasurable and a lot of people don't frown upon. Like sex with your spouse.

I'm talking about that other kind of sex—extramarital sex, premarital sex, sex that will get you on the Oprah Winfrey show, like sex on a UFO or with a famous politician.

I know you're asking, but how would the government be able

to collect a fooling-around tax? People simply wouldn't admit to such a thing.

Okay, I don't have all the details worked out yet. Maybe we could appeal to people's egos. You put out a tax form that says, "How much illicit sex did you have last year?" and what stud wannabe, or otherwise, is going to put down "I went scoreless."

Some might even exaggerate in an attempt to advertise their sexual prowess at their local IRS office.

Whatever, it's an idea that has merit because, I firmly believe, a lot more people fool around these days than smoke. You never see a sign in an office building that says, "Thank you for not fooling around."

You probably could have sex at a hockey game and get away with it, but light up in a federal building and they'll call the SWAT team.

Of course, there are different levels of recreational sex and different ways of engaging in it.

Under my plan, how much fooling-around tax you pay would depend on these differentials.

For example:

If you did it in a mobile home, you obviously didn't get filthy rich in the Reagan-Bush era, so you don't have to pay as much as, say, someone who was able to pop for a suite at the Ritz and designer condoms with polo players on them.

If you did it in a private jet you would be taxed at a higher rate than someone fooling around in a van with a bumper sticker that reads, IF THIS VAN IS ROCKIN', DON'T COME KNOCKIN'.

If your partner dressed up like a duck it would cost you more if he or she actually made quacking sounds.

If you used whips and/or chains you would pay a 10 percent

surcharge, but you would have your health card to get treatment for any injuries incurred.

If any video equipment was employed, there would also be a 10 percent surcharge, but you would be free to sell any tapes to Oprah, her highest-bidding competitor, or the famous politician you have on tape chasing you around the room while quacking like a duck.

If Heidi Fleiss was involved in any way, you'll be taxed 15 percent of what you gross out of your next movie, docudrama, or presidential haircut.

If Conan O'Brien was involved, who cares?

Members of the American Association of Retired Persons would receive reduced rates, as well as no charge for vibrating mattresses at motels.

Faked orgasms are on the house.

Ask not who you can do, my fellow Americans, but who you can do for your country.

Correctly Spoken

YELLOW SPRINGS, OHIO—Antioch College's new rules to tell when a yes is a yes and not a no:

"May I hold your hand?"

"May you do what?"

"May I hold your hand?"

"How do you mean that?"

"I just mean I would like to hold your hand, but, under the new campus regulations, I need to get your explicit permission before I can do it."

"You want to put your flesh on my flesh, am I correct?"

"I wouldn't exactly put it that way."

"Well, how would you put it?"

"I just thought since we've been seeing each other for three months and I've never held your hand, I'd like to."

"I see. You want to press your bare skin against my bare skin."

"I never said anything about that. I'm just asking if it would be okay with you if we held hands."

"Pervert."

"Okay, forget holding hands. Do you mind if I gaze into your eyes?"

"What kind of sicko thing is that?"

"I just think you have lovely eyes and I thought it would be romantic to gaze into them."

"I know what's on your mind. You want to gaze into my eyes and hypnotize me and then hold my hand."

"No, it's just that we're all alone and it's a lovely night, and I thought I might gaze into your eyes and tell you what I feel."

"Want to cop a feel, do you? You're getting real close to a date in court, buster."

"Forget gazing into your eyes. May I whisper sweet nothings into your ear?"

"Stay away from my ear."

"I just want to whisper into it."

"Whisper into your own ear, you creep, or I start screaming. What kind of woman do you take me for?"

"How about if I recite you a love poem?"

"You want to try to titillate me with filthy literature, don't you? You saw what happened to Clarence Thomas when he tried that?"

"I was thinking of something perhaps from Omar Khayyam."

"Who is he? The screenwriter for Long Dong Silver?"

"Of course not. He wrote beautiful love poems."

"I'm calling a campus cop."

"May I serenade you with a love song then?"

"Fiend."

"How about 'The Shadow of Your Smile'?"

"One note and I knee you!"

"Then may I tell you how lovely you look in the moonlight?"

"You're trying to look through my blouse, aren't you?"

"No. I just mean that when the moonlight hits your hair, it reminds me of a thousand stars glimmering off the water."

"You filthy-mouthed sleezeball!"

"May I take you on a romantic stroll through the campus?"

"You're not getting me in the dark."

"That's not what I had in mind at all. I just thought we could go for a little walk and perhaps I could get to know you better."

"Know me? I've read the Bible, you lecherous, drooling sodomite."

"It's cool out. Would you like to wear my jacket?"

"Cross-dresser, huh? Feckless kinkophile!"

"Mind if I loosen my tie?"

"Brazen exhibitionist!"

"Look, Hilda, wanna get a motel room and have sex?"

"I thought you'd never ask."

7 CULTURE

For Those Who Call Spaghetti Pasta

Say It Ain't So, Buffalo Bob

I've never cared much for the artsy crowd. They hold too many benefits, for one thing.

For another, they are the kind of people who would look at a photograph or a painting of a cat nailed to a telephone pole and say, "My, look at those lines," if it were hanging in a museum and somebody told them it was art.

The rest of us, of course, would say, "Good God. It's a cat nailed to a telephone pole. I think I'm going to be sick."

The artsy crowd currently is flitting about with great concern because of what it considers to be an effort by uncultured imbeciles to censor certain works it contends are not obscene, but of great artistic value.

There was Cincinnati, where a museum showed photographs taken by somebody named Robert Mapplethorpe.

The photographs were quite explicit. The artsy crowd looked at them and said, "My, look at those lines."

Others said, "Good God. I think I'm going to be sick."

A trial was held to decide whether or not a museum had the right to show the photographs.

The artsy crowd won, and if I had been on the jury, I would

have cast my vote for allowing the museum to show anything it pleases, too.

Censorship in any form is wrong.

But that opinion doesn't stop me from saying that what's basically wrong with the artsy crowd is, it's full of it.

Sure, offer the photographs for those who want to gaze upon such. But don't try to pass it off as art.

One of the photographs in question was of a man with a bullwhip in his rectum.

During the Cincinnati trial the prosecutor asked the art director, who selected the photographs for the show, if he thought it depicted sexuality.

No, said the art director, it was a figure study.

Bullsomething else.

What it was was a photograph of a man with a bullwhip in his rectum, and no matter what the artsy crowd might call it, it's still a photograph of a man with a bullwhip in his rectum.

Doesn't common sense tell those people that?

Again, I'm not for censoring such a photograph. I'm just saying it's sleazy, filthy, obscene, decadent, and sick, and anybody who would call it otherwise is a damn fool.

At the recent Atlanta Arts Festival there was a puppet show, and at one point during the act, the puppets depicted oral sex.

Say it ain't so, Buffalo Bob. Puppets having oral sex and a photograph of a man with a bullwhip in his rectum.

If the artsy crowd doesn't awaken to the fact the rest of society isn't going to stop crying "smut" at such, then public support of the worthwhile might eventually stop, too.

The point here is, the artsy crowd can stick a bullwhip in its rectum and call it macaroni or anything else it wants to. Anything else but art.

At least we uncultured imbeciles recognize an old-fashioned maggot-gagger when we see one.

My Night at the Opera

A number of my uncultured friends have been giving me the business about attending the opera recently, the same evening of a Braves-Giants baseball game the sportswriters called the most important regular-season Atlanta game since the beginning of time.

Naturally, I have not allowed this criticism to bother me. I would not have thought of missing the opening of the Atlanta Opera Company's *La Bohème* for something as pedestrian as a baseball game.

Besides, I couldn't get tickets to the ball game. A couple of forty-eight-dollar back-row seats for *La Bohème* were a cinch.

"The game was on TV," said my friends, who think opera is for people who call spaghetti pasta.

I even had to drag my lovely fiancée, Dedra, to the performance. She wanted to stay home and read the latest John Grisham legal novel, *The Bill*.

"You'll love the opera," I said. "*La Bohème* is very romantic."

"That's what you said about the Citrus Bowl," she argued.

Some people, like me, are born to culture. Others have it thrust upon them. That's what Richard Gere said to Julia Roberts, by the way, when he took her to see the opera in *Pretty Woman*, where she wet her britches. I mean, she liked it better than *Rags to Riches*. (Editor's note: A TV comedy/drama series that ran from March 1987 to September 1988.)

La Bohème is about a sick girl who dies. She coughs a lot in the first three acts and then dies in the fourth.

The thing about opera, however, is a cough can last fifteen minutes.

This wasn't my first opera. I attended the opera once in Vienna. That opera was about everybody wanting to go to bed with the plump chambermaid.

There were differences between the Vienna opera and the Atlanta opera.

In Vienna the hall wasn't air-conditioned. The plump chambermaid looked like she'd been through two IRS audits by the end of the performance.

It was quite comfortable, however, in Atlanta's Symphony Hall. Put on an opera in Atlanta in early September in a building that isn't air-conditioned and the joint would smell like Ron Gant's socks after a doubleheader.

What else was different was there was a screen above the stage in Atlanta that offered English subtitles. That's how I learned an operatic cough could last fifteen minutes.

A man sang and sang and sang to the sick girl. The screen flashed what he said in English, which came out, "You okay?"

She replied for fifteen minutes, hitting notes that could have thrown Delta flights landing at Hartsfield off course, and, at the end, the screen flashed "Haaaaack!"

To be perfectly honest about it, I was a bit embarrassed for my hometown. I thought showing English subtitles at the opera was saying to us, "We know you rubes have no idea what's going on here, so we'll make it easy for you."

I, of course, didn't need them.

In *The Godfather,* for instance, somebody rambled on for fifteen minutes in Italian, and I knew what he had said was "Cut off the horse's head and put it in the creep's bed."

Something else embarrassed me, too. There were many Atlanta opera-goers who sat there with plugs in their ears listening to radios.

Just before the sick girl died, a lot of them cheered.

"They shouldn't cheer anybody dying," said Dedra.

"They're not," I said. "I think the Braves just scored."

Imagine people sitting at an opera listening to a baseball game. Especially when they paid forty-eight dollars to see what amounted to a Vicks commercial.

But Is It Art?

The latest example of how the National Endowment for the Arts wastes your tax money comes from three experimental artists in California.

They received a $5,000 grant from the NEA, cashed it into ten-dollar bills and gave them away to illegal immigrants.

What's that got to do with art?

According to an article I read, ". . . to David Avalos, one of the artists, the act of giving the money is a work of art and a political statement about 'the interaction of physical space with intellectual space and civic space.' "

A reporter watching this "work of art" reported many of the illegal immigrants immediately went to a nearby lunch stand and bought soft drinks and tacos with their ten-dollar bills.

However, we finally got some public awareness of just what a crock the NEA is and how it respects tax dollars as if they were mere taco mixings.

Never being one not to add fuel where there's a good fire, I have obtained a list of other recent grants for artists in this country through my many Washington sources. Thought you might like to know:

Grover (Pierre) Turnipseed of Boaz, Ala., recently received a

$10,000 grant to do a photographic display of tobacco spit he found in the parking lot of various truck stops around the state.

The display, incidentally, is titled "Jus."

Danielle Throckmorton-Haliburton of St. Paul, Minn., pocketed a $27,000 grant to choreograph an original dance dedicated to the former Hooters waitresses in Atlanta currently suing the company on sexual-harassment charges.

Titled "The Hoot Scoot for Loot," the dance will be performed by the artist for an upcoming American Bar Association convention.

Mervin Pitts of Bismarck, N.D., was given a $150,000 award to build a scale replica of the carvings on Mount Rushmore out of one box of hog pellets. Mr. Pitts reports he might put President Clinton's face on his piece of art but he's not sure which one.

Sonya Shacklejaw of Taos, N.M., got 32,000 big ones for a documentary on the sexual-harassment tactics of the male porcupine. It's titled "Porky."

(Believe me, the one-word title of the film is a lot less offensive than the "Piss Christ" photograph or the photo of the male with the bullwhip in his rectum, also brought to you by the NEA.)

Loody Hogarth of Columbia, S.C., took home $161,000 for an exhibit of the really cute sugar-sprinkle designs she and her nine-year-old daughter, Vanessa, put on some donuts. Vanessa received a similar grant last year for a study on what would happen if her late four-year-old brother ate all her finger paints.

Shirley Finkleheimer of Dallas, Texas, got $20,000 for an oil painting of the wart on the end of her nose. The White House was so impressed, Ms. Finkleheimer has been commissioned to paint Hillary Clinton wearing a pair of her husband's boxer shorts.

Garth Milldew of Des Moines, Iowa, was given $1.5 million to write obscene poems on men's room walls in various Midwestern truck stops.

Norbert Gooch, Brooklyn, N.Y., received $27,500 to doodle on the back of a box of Argo starch while having phone sex with a talking chicken.

Feel like somebody just stuck you with a bullwhip? Somebody did.

Country Music—
That's My Thang

Even if you don't particularly enjoy country music, you've got to admit some of the titles, lyrics and thoughts are wonderfully poetic.

For years, there was something that circulated called "The List." It included the very best country music titles and lyrics. Remember these titles?:

"My Wife Just Ran Off with My Best Friend, and I Miss Him."

"I Gave Her a Ring and She Gave Me a Finger."

"We Used to Kiss on the Lips, But It's All Over Now."

"Every Man Must Leave His Footprints in the Shifting Sands of Time, But I'll Just Leave the Mark of a Heel."

"How Come My Dog Don't Bark When You Come Around?"

"I've Got Tears in My Ears from Lying on My Back Crying All Night Over You."

And these equally impressive lyrics?:

"If your phone don't ring, it's me."

"Ain't only one thing in this ol' world worth a solitary dime, and that's old dogs, and children, and watermelon wine."

"If you're waitin' on me, you're backin' up."

"Has anybody here seen my sweet thang?"

"The work we did, it was hard, but we slept at night cause we was tard." (That may be a paraphrase, but it's close enough— from Loretta Lynn's "Coal Miner's Daughter.")

Country music can be used in real-life situations. A friend was telling me how, when he asked his wife for a divorce, she refused and demanded they go to a marriage counselor.

At the last session with the counselor, the counselor asked my friend's wife, "Is there any song that really sums up your feelings for your husband?"

She responded, "Each time I hear Johnny Mathis sing 'Until the Twelfth of Never,' I think of him."

"And what about you?" the counselor asked my friend. "Is there any particular song that sums up your feelings for your wife?"

"Absolutely," he replied. "Roy Clark's immortal 'Thank God and Greyhound She's Gone.'"

My friend got his divorce.

I bring all this up because of a country song I heard recently by George Jones. For those who are not familiar with Mr. Jones, he's been around for years and is a notorious drinker.

On one occasion his former wife, country singer Tammy Wynette, left their Nashville home to go on tour. She had all the liquor removed from the house, and left George with no car.

No problem for George. He was last seen heading to the nearest bar, driving the couple's lawn mower.

Despite his drinking problems, George Jones is recognized by many as the best country singer ever. His voice has the same tone as a steel guitar when he sings of love—lost and found.

And his latest: There's this guy, and his baby has gone, and he's sitting at home and darkness has come and he's got the hurt-all-over blues.

He turns to drink as the answer. He pulls off the shelf a decanter of bourbon that is in the image of the late Elvis. He's got to have something to drink the bourbon from, so he locates a Fred Flintstone jelly jar.

He pours out the jelly, steams the label off the jar and pours himself a drink out of Elvis.

And he sings:

"Yabba Dabba Doo, the King is gone, and so are you."

A classic is born.

8 MEDIA

A Local Yokel
in Search of (Gasp)
the Truth

Entertainment Without the Raunch

The television remote control device is one of the few things mechanical or electronic I can successfully operate.

By that I mean I can turn the television on, I can turn it off, I can control the volume and I can switch the channels.

It is also one of the few modern conveniences I consider a true convenience.

The electric toothbrush certainly isn't. Somebody gave me one of those. I put the toothpaste on the brush, but when I hit the juice, the brush vibrates so violently by the time I get it to my mouth, it has shaken the toothpaste off. Toothpaste in your eyes burns.

The automatic coffee maker really isn't automatic. If it were automatic it would locate those little packs of coffee I can never find in my kitchen and then pour the water in itself.

Do you realize what we had to do before we had those remote magic clickers?

We actually had to get up off our rears, walk over to the set and manually turn the channel changer.

Had it not been for the magic clicker, I wouldn't have had the warm, wonderful experience I had recently.

I had retired early and turned on the television in my bedroom.

"I'll lie here," I said to myself, "and watch a good movie."

I knew I could use the magic clicker to find one. I wouldn't have to jump up and out of bed, switching channels in my search.

I began at the lower end of the channel range, where HBO is and Cinemax and the Movie Channel are located.

On one, fourteen people were shooting automatic weapons at one another. Blood was gushing. I hit the magic clicker.

On the next channel, a man and a woman were engaged in heated dialogue. In thirty seconds they each used the "f" word in a veritable buffet of variations. There was a time you couldn't say "pregnant" on television.

On to the third channel. Jim and Margaret Anderson didn't even sleep together on *Father Knows Best*. There was enough skin showing in the first thirty seconds of the movie showing on this particular channel to reupholster an entire Greyhound bus.

So on I went. Through the mindless sitcoms of the network channels. Through CNN and war and famine and disease and Hillary. Through TNN and men in cowboy hats line-dancing with women in dire need of NordicTracks.

And, then, to TNT. They were showing Lassie movies on TNT. Can you imagine that? In the quagmire of sex and violence, midst the medium that spawned Beavis and Butt-head and rock videos and the ever-increasing innuendos of the sitcoms, I found Lassie.

What I watched, in its entirety, was *Son of Lassie*, colorized, but otherwise as pure as ever.

Peter Lawford, of all people, was an RAF pilot and he was shot down behind Nazi lines with Laddie, Lassie's own.

They become separated and Laddie goes on the inevitable search to find his master. There were fresh-faced, laughing children in the movie and good people fighting evil and one determined dog.

It was my best television moment since Aunt Bee went to Mt. Pilot and Andy and Opie made her feel unneeded by keeping the house spotless while she was away.

Nobody used the "f" word. Nobody blew off anybody else's head. Nobody got naked.

It's still in that box, though limited: entertainment without the raunch. You just have to look for it, and the magic clicker, bless it, puts it at your fingertips.

See Laddie run. I dreamt that night the Beav and I went spitting off a bridge.

And Now, a Word from . . .

ATLANTA—A couple of Atlanta television stations this fall decided not to run any political advertisements during the city elections.

Perhaps they figured they give us enough drivel with the lineup of network programming they cast upon us.

Whatever the reason, they are to be commended. Think of what we were spared:

"My opponent wears smelly socks, kidnaps little puppies and eats raw wienies."

"That's nothing. My opponent sucks eggs, runs rabbits, and doesn't close his eyes during prayer."

"You think that's disgusting. The idiot running against me has a wart on his nose, supports thespianism and sold Kool-Aid to Jim Jones."

If only television stations could be convinced to become more discerning toward all sorts of commercials, not just those of a political nature.

I made a list of the sort of television commercials I despise the most, and in a perfect world, I would never have to see them again.

Here is my list:

AUTOMOBILE COMMERCIALS: "Hey, we're giving these cars away! No, we'll pay you to take them off our hands!"

I actually come from a long line of used-car dealers and horse thieves, but local car dealers have no business doing their own commercials on television. They are loud, they are obnoxious and they kidnap little puppies. Call BR 549 if you agree.

CEREAL COMMERCIALS: There simply can't be that much difference among cereals. Muleslick, or whatever it's called, can't be any better friend to your colon than Bowel Bran. Can it?

Of course it can't. And, furthermore, I don't care if cereal becomes soggy, that's why I put milk in it. Bowel Bran today. Can Tree Bark be far behind?

FEMININE HYGIENE PRODUCTS: I'll keep this simple and discreet. I don't care if it will hold and absorb the entire Atlantic

Ocean, I don't want to have to sit in my den and hear about it on my television.

DIARRHEA AND CONSTIPATION COMMERCIALS: This family goes to Hawaii and they all come down with diarrhea and can't get out of their room. It happens.

But I don't care. Just pretend you're doing the hula and find a facility.

PERFUME AND COLOGNE COMMERCIALS: I could abide these if they made any sense. But they rarely do. There's a naked couple, except for sunglasses, riding orangutans through a field of nuclear waste, and it's a commercial about a new cologne named "Goat Sweat."

A man likes to smell like a man. A woman like a woman. Not a bodily function or the scent of the North Dakota female doodlebug in heat.

LAWYER COMMERCIALS: Every ambulance chaser in the country has his or her own television commercial. "The law firm of Loophole and Whiplash will sue anybody, living or dead, for the low, low price of $29.95. Judge Wapner is our first cousin, by the way, and we've read all the John Grisham novels. Trust us."

Yeah, and those law books behind you were painted on the walls. Go for a court-appointed attorney and hope he or she doesn't stutter.

PET FOOD COMMERCIALS: "This dog food is beefy and chewy tasting." How does the announcer know that? The dog didn't tell him.

HAIR COMMERCIALS: If God hadn't wanted you to be bald, you'd have been born with a cat on your head.

Get rid of insurance commercials featuring aging actors and stop telling me that Juan Valdez is from Colombia. We're supposed to believe he's got coffee in those sacks?

So many bad commercials. So little space.

Unsophisticated in Reagansville

WASHINGTON—Public television was doing a series of programs entitled *Back of the Book* in which various individuals were to sit around a table and discuss matters pertaining to books, movies, television, music and the media.

The group invited to Washington to participate included:

- The rock music critic of *Rolling Stone*.
- The television critic of the *Chicago Tribune*, a woman.
- An editor from *Adweek*, also a woman, who agreed with most everything the lady TV critic from Chicago said.
- An erudite professor from Amherst, where the debate team probably gets more attention than the football squad.
- The movie critic of *The Washington Post*, who wears glasses with red rims.
- A man from Chicago who identified himself as a "political satirist." Great work, I suppose, if you can get it.
- And me.

I wasn't certain why I had been asked to take part in the discussions, but when I told the TV critic from Chicago I lived in Atlanta, was a graduate of the University of Georgia and thought George Jones was the best thing to come along since sliced bread, she said, "Oh, then you must be our local yokel."

That was my first clue I probably wasn't going to fit in here. For the next three days, I went head to head with this group of sophisticates, none of whom ever agreed with a single thing I said. I haven't felt that out of place since I walked into Brooks Brothers looking for a pair of jeans.

We were talking about subway vigilante Bernhard Goetz, for instance. Everybody else said they thought he was sick and should be put under the jail.

I said I thought he was a great American hero for striking back against crime and that Roy Rogers would have done the same thing if four thugs had messed with him on a subway. You should have heard their howls of disgust.

We talked about *The New Yorker* magazine. The professor from Amherst said anybody who didn't read it probably attended the University of Georgia.

I said I didn't think it was so hot because I went to a cocktail party given by *The New Yorker* once and they didn't have any beer. All they served was white wine, which I pointed out is the favorite drink of wimps and feminists with chips on their shoulders.

We talked about our favorite movies. Somebody said theirs was Rainer Werner Fassbinder's immortal *Marriage of Maria Braun*.

I said mine was *Walking Tall*, where Joe Don Baker takes apart a bar with a big stick. I thought the movie critic from the *Post* was going to faint.

We also discussed the explicit lyrics of rock star Prince. The man from *Rolling Stone* said that's just the way young people are these days. I said the only good thing about Prince is now we don't have to spend a lot of tax money on sex education in our schools. Just give every kid a Prince album.

Finally, the moderator asked each member of the panel for any closing thoughts.

My fellow panel members discussed all sorts of issues I didn't understand and the professor from Amherst said that anybody who would drink beer at a *New Yorker* cocktail party wasn't socially fit to attend a hog-slopping.

When it came my turn, I said, "How about them Dawgs!" and caught the first bus home.

Cracking Down on the Speech Police

A lot of activists have beards. Even female activists. Most of them have educations, but many of them have been educated beyond their intelligence.

Add all these people together, and they amount to a minuscule percentage of the entire population, but that doesn't matter. Since they control all the newspapers and television networks, they also have the floor at all times, and the rest of us never get a chance to be recognized.

But one might ask, "What about conservative politicians? Can't and don't they ever speak out?" Oh, one might slip and say he or she doesn't believe in racial quotas and suggest the welfare system needs changing, but the *Times* et al. will scream, and an aide to the politician will say, "I don't care if that's the way you feel. You just can't say things like that anymore."

That's what the Speech Police finally have done. They have made the American tradition of speaking one's mind almost a hanging offense.

"But what if one speaks his mind and it happens to be the truth?"

The *truth*? What's the truth got to do with anything?

How the Speech Police managed to deal with truth is they started something called *political correctness*, which is fairly simple to define. It means *keep your mouth shut, even if it is true, because we don't care about truth anymore.* What if somebody asks you, "What do you think of welfare mothers who continue to have babies out of wedlock because they can get more benefits that way?" The truthful way to answer is by saying, "To hell with 'em. The welfare system is completely out of control, and although I certainly believe in helping people if they really need it, I also believe there are many instances of welfare cheating, and as long as welfare is available, it will, in fact, zap the ambition for some to go out and see if they can find a job. Plus, the government is going broke trying to pay for it."

That's the truth, but it's not politically correct.

The best way to answer is first to ask a question: "How many babies are we talking about a welfare mother having out of wedlock?"

And let's say the answer is "Oh, about seventeen."

The politically correct answer would be, then, "The government should buy her a roomier Cadillac."

Here are some other things you can't say if you want to be politically correct, regardless of whether or not they are true:

- "If male homosexuals would stop having unprotected anal sex with one another, it probably would go a long way in helping stem the rising tide of AIDS cases."
- "The Rev. Al Sharpton is an opportunist who looks like Fats Domino with a Prince Valiant haircut."
- "I pulled for Clarence Thomas."
- "I wouldn't pee on Ted Kennedy's leg if he was on fire."
- "I think women who don't shave their legs aren't sexy."
- "Look at where all the racial strife is now—New York. People have learned to get along in Mississippi."
- "Goddamn sneaky Japs. I still don't trust 'em."
- "Is Pat Schroeder a pain in the ass, or what?"
- "Just because one group happened to do poorer on a test than another group, I don't think we should make the test easier for the group that did the poorest. Why don't we keep the test the same and figure out a way to smarten up the group that came in second?"
- "I thought *Grand Canyon* sucked."
- "Jesus, I'm tired of hearing about the plight of the black athlete. How much does Michael Jordan make a year anyway?"
- "My wife found some old *Amos and Andy* tapes and gave them to me for Christmas. Boy, I'd forgotten just how funny that was. I don't understand why they can't bring them back. What's the difference between Fred Sanford and Kingfish?"
- "Why don't they make golf courses just for women? They could take all day playing, and nobody would give a damn."

- "If they can pick a black (African-American) All-American team, why can't they pick a white All-American team?"
- "Damn, I'm sick of the federal government telling me I've got to hire some idiot who doesn't know his ass from third base just because he's [fill in the blank]."
- "I worked sixteen hours a day, seven days a week, for years until I finally made it. Why should the government take my hard-earned money to pay some son of a bitch who is too lazy to work?"
- "You know, a lot of things David Duke said made sense."
- "Crank up the *Enola Gay.*"

Say anything like any of that, and you are politically incorrect, which also means you are racist, sexist, homophobic, etc., and you also probably are for giving drug traffickers the death penalty.

Political correctness also means changing a few ideas about history. Christopher Columbus is no longer a brave explorer, for instance. He's a rotten white guy who introduced all sorts of disease to the New World he discovered, and he should be erased from the history books and more attention should be given to Afrocentrism, which is about civilization beginning in Africa, where it was later introduced to the Greeks by soul singer James Brown, who was wrongly incarcerated several thousand years later by racist South Carolina law-enforcement officers who didn't realize the reason James was doing all that dope and trying to outrun them at 110 miles per hour was to protest there aren't any African-Americans in the National Hockey League.

That's basically a politically correct history of the world, except you need to throw in that Plato and Socrates were homosexual lovers, God is a black woman, and the Devil is a white guy who belonged to the all-white Kappa Alpha fraternity when he was an undergraduate at the University of Alabama.

In order to be politically correct, it is also necessary to know the correct term to use when referring to certain groups who are very touchy about things like that.

If you're still saying "black," you're wrong. It's African-American now, and don't dare mention that the C in NAACP still stands for you-know-what.

Indians are not Indians anymore. They are Native Americans, despite the fact America got its name from an Italian.

"Gay" and "homosexual" may even be on the way out. Soon, one might be asked to say "individuals exercising their right to engage in an alternative lifestyle."

Then, you get into your other So-and-so-Americans like Italians, Hispanic, etc., except you never refer to anybody whose forebears came from say, England, because English-Americans are all a bunch of rich Protestant white people who have all the money and good jobs and got them by kicking around everybody else.

Where a white guy gets into trouble the most often is when he refers to the gender that isn't male. That gender used to be called "female." But "female" is out, because the word "male" is in there, so how about "feperson"? How about "women"? No, that has "men" in it. Some members of the Speech Police are saying it's okay to say that word, as long as you spell it "womyn." So is a "hysterectomy" a "herterectomy" now? If you read about Catherine the Great are you reading about Russian herstory?

To be completely politically correct, should men say, instead of "Look at that womyn over there," "Look at the individual who is certainly my equal in each and every way over there"?

We've gone way beyond the old "Miss," "Ms.," and "Mrs." debate. I found out something else, too. Never call a trumpet player a "lady." Here's what happened to me:

The Atlanta Braves, woeful since back when you still said you were "shacked up with your main squeeze" instead of today's politically correct "cohabitating with your significant other," won the 1992 National League Baseball Pennant. The Braves hosted their first World Series in mid-October, and I was there on assignment for my newspaper, to columnize about what I saw and felt on this historic (herstoric) occasion.

When it came time for the national anthem, the stadium announcer said a trumpet player from the St. Louis Symphony would do the honors.

I began to think, which I shouldn't have. Start thinking in these times and you simply don't know where it could lead.

My first thought was, "Why is a trumpet player from the St. Louis Symphony doing the national anthem at the first World Series game ever played in Atlanta?"

Wasn't there anybody from Atlanta who could have played the national anthem? I felt bringing in an outsider was both inappropriate and an affront. This was Atlanta's finest hour. The person from St. Louis who played the anthem happened to be a *womyn*. The reason I knew that was because the stadium announcer had called her name, and it was something like "Delores." Also, I could see her on the field.

After the game, I wrote something like "At 8:42, a trumpet player from the St. Louis Symphony, a lady, played the national anthem. I'm not sure why."

I admit it was a lazy paragraph. In the first place, I should have asked somebody who might have known why somebody from St. Louis was playing the national anthem at Atlanta's first home World Series game. I would have found out, as I did later, Major League Baseball, not the Braves, decides who's going to play the national anthem at World Series games, and perhaps somebody in on that decision-making arm owed something to said trumpet player.

Where I made my big mistake, however, was identifying the trumpet player as "a lady." Local feminist members of the Speech Police barraged me the next few days with letters and telephone calls, and threatened the continued health of my testicles.

I was berated and called a Neanderthal because these women said it was a dirty, rotten sexist thing to do to identify the gender of the trumpet player.

Some of the letters and calls also said I was being patronizing for using the term "lady."

I didn't understand. Weren't we taught at journalism school about giving all the details in a story? The trumpet player had, in fact, been a womyn. I was simply stating a fact. A *truth*, that pesky word again.

According to the letters and calls, however, here was why I was politically incorrect for identifying the gender of the trumpet player. Wrote one irate "individual who is [my] equal, etc.":

"If the trumpet player had been a male, would you have written 'A trumpet player, etc., a gentleman, . . . ?' Of course you wouldn't. But you found it somehow strange a woman would be playing the trumpet at a baseball game, and by using the term 'lady' you expressed that feeling. The fact is, women can play a trumpet just as well as men."

I certainly never meant to imply such a thing, although if there would have even been a Battle of the Sexes in trumpet playing back when Louis Armstrong was still alive, I'd have taken him over any trumpet player the National Organization of Women might have entered.

I actually went as far as to call a spokes-Ms. at *Ms.* magazine for further enlightenment. I was told basically the same thing the letter-writers and callers said. I was politically incorrect for identifying the gender of the trumpet player. I was also told "lady" is no longer an operable term, as when a womyn drives into a mechanic shop with a broken muffler, and Leroy, the head mechanic, greets her by saying, "What can I do for you, little lady?"

I wrote somewhat of an apology in a subsequent column, pleading ignorance to all the rules of political correctness. After that, I got an equal amount of calls and letters from men saying I had betrayed them by apologizing. I also got a few calls and letters from the other gender (and I'm not implying anything by saying "the other gender," I just couldn't think of any other way to say it) indicating they still liked to be called "a lady." But these women likely still make the coffee for their male bosses each morning.

Perhaps some sort of disclaimer is necessary at this point. I know if this book is reviewed by anybody for the *Times* or the *Post* they will skip right over this, but I'm going to say it anyway:

1. I don't want to put black people in the back of the bus again. The civil-rights movement was the right thing to do, and the courage of those involved set an example for all humanity.

But I'm tired of racism as an excuse. More black men are in jail than in college. Black leaders blame white people for that, and as long as there is somebody else to blame, nothing gets done about a problem.

Black politicians get caught stealing. It's a racist plot, somebody cries. And there's a subsequent rally at the First Ebenezer

Baptist Church, where supporters of the politicians get together and shout racism in unison. They also wind up on the news and in the papers the next day.

Marion Barry? It was white people who put that cocaine in his pipe. Richard Arrington, mayor of Birmingham? He didn't do anything wrong. Because we're talking about Birmingham, as in Alabama, Selma, the South, the fire hoses, dogs, Rosa Parks, and Bull Connor. Another racist scheme to bring down black leaders.

Hosea Williams, an old civil-rights war-horse, has been a one-man traffic hazard in Atlanta for years. We're talking everything from DUI to hit-and-run. Hosea said a lot of his problems with the Atlanta police dated back to the time he tried to get a white police chief thrown out. Another racist plot.

And does the fact there hasn't *been* a white police chief in Atlanta in decades muddy Hosea's credibility? It does with me.

Racism is such a convenient excuse. Get caught and you can always explain it away. The truth is, some black politicians steal, just like some white politicians.

I used to play a lot of tennis, but my right arm fell off as a result, so I had to quit. Several years ago, I was playing in a tournament and drew an opponent who happened to be black. At the end of one rally, he hit a ball that was wide by a good five feet. I called it out.

He called me a racist.

Racism will never die, indeed, until it ceases to be used.

2. If a womyn, or whatever I'm supposed to call them, can do the job of a man, she should be given an equal chance to get that job and receive the same pay as a man would receive if he held the position. I still have a little problem with women on the golf course who will keep hitting the ball until they get it into

the hole, instead of picking up and moving to the next hole when they reach double or triple bogey, as golf's handicap system provides, but that's a minor thing compared to the larger question of women's rights in the workplace.

3. Homosexuality really doesn't bother me until it spills into the streets or is flaunted at me. I sort of feel the same way about heterosexuality, although not as strongly. God gave us the motel room so we wouldn't do things like that.

But political correctness has gotten out of hand. The Speech Police have gotten out of hand. They are stifling expression. It used to take me, say, an hour to write a newspaper column, once I settled on the idea and decided not to be embarrassed about it. Today, I must search deep for any insensitivities in each sentence, each word. Politicians have to be wary of each statement they utter, lest some group become aroused and they have to go on the nightly news and say, "I regret referring to [name it] as [name it]." Politicians were sidesteppers nonpareil as it was.

Lord knows, there is such a thing as good taste and manners. And there is also such a thing as individuals holding lofty positions using some judgment. As much as I abhor the Speech Police, I certainly don't want the president of the United States opening his press conferences by telling divisive racial jokes.

Don Rickles is the only white person who can still get away with using racial humor, for some reason I don't understand. The president can't do it. Unless we have a black president one day. Then, he or she can make fun of white people drinking Tab and wearing weird clothes when they play golf.

9 POLITICS

Nuke the Gay Whales for Jesus

Right, Not Wrong

I need to explain my politics and exactly what I would do if I were president. You can learn an awful lot why a person says and acts the way he or she says and acts by learning of their politics and exactly what they would do if they were president.

First, my politics. It's like a friend of mine explaining what to do when you are faced with which way to turn. He said, "Always go right. If you go left, you can never go right, and if you go right, you can never go wrong."

Right is where I am on the political spectrum. The only good liberal is one who has been thrown out of office or is up in Alaska somewhere trying to save the whales and isn't around to get on my very last nerve.

You want to know just how right I am? Okay, let's take some key issues of today, and I'll tell you where I stand on them.

In no particular order, then:

WELFARE: I'm against it. I explain how to take care of people who are truly needy somewhere else in this book, but I can't remember exactly where.

IMMIGRATION: America first, with apologies to one of my heroes, Pat Buchanan.

TRADE BARRIERS: Tell the Japs if they try to sell one more Toyota, we're cranking up the *Enola Gay* again. We need to continue to trade with England, however, because I own a Jaguar and might need some parts. As far as the Germans are concerned, I don't like German wines, and I got rid of my two-seater Mercedes convertible.

I also figure we can make our own vodka, and there's nothing else in Name du Jour (formerly the Soviet Union) worth having. I've been there. Trust me. The same goes for France and their wines. And their food always has too much sauce on it.

As far as Italy is concerned, I do have a certain fondness for Gucci shoes, but I wore Bass Weejuns exclusively for years, and I can go back to them.

And North Korea can just plain kiss my butt, and I wear an American-made watch, so that's it for the Swiss. I could go on, but you should have my bent on this issue by now.

Meanwhile, allow American producers to sell anywhere to whoever'll buy whatever we're selling, which also brings up foreign aid.

FOREIGN AID: Give everybody in the world who is starving some food. If one of our friends needs some weapons to battle one of our enemies, we get Schwarzkopf and go in and blow away the enemy of our friends ourselves. Cut out the middleman.

TAX INCENTIVES FOR THE RICH: You saw what happened with the liberals' stupid luxury tax, didn't you? It was a way to get the rich, but it didn't. The luxury tax on boats, for instance, was so high, rich people didn't buy any boats, so the boat industry went to hell and put a lot of people out of work.

We ought to keep the rich as rich as possible, because nobody poor was ever able to afford to give anybody else a job.

DEFENSE: Stay strong. I don't trust anybody.

QUOTAS: No, but I do wonder why there aren't more black hockey players and so few Jewish country-music singers.

THE ENVIRONMENT: Put a tent over Los Angeles so whatever it is they breathe out there doesn't spread to the rest of the country. Close New Jersey. Protect the water. If there is any way to save a tree when bulldozing for a new condominium complex, do it, but don't spend a lot of money trying to save the snail darter. Move the hole in the ozone layer over Chicago so the people who live there can warm up for once in their lives. Leave the fishermen alone. We can always eat baloney if we run out of fish.

CAPITAL PUNISHMENT: I'm for it. Not a single person ever executed for murder committed another one.

PRAYER IN THE SCHOOLS: Bring it back. Just don't paddle a kid for kicking another kid in the shins while the prayer is going on. I wonder if my fifth-grade teacher, Mrs. Covin, still remembers that incident?

ALL-MALE GOLF CLUBS: Yes, yes!

ALL-FEMALE GOLF CLUBS: The holes would be too short for a long hitter like me, so go right ahead, ladies.

ALL-ANYTHING-ELSE COUNTRY CLUBS: I'm big on the right to privacy.

THE HIGH COST OF HEALTH CARE: Just try not to get sick until somebody thinks of something.

BUMPER STICKER I'M GOING TO PUT ON MY CAR: NUKE THE GAY WHALES FOR JESUS.

Too Old to Drink?

If the federal government really wants to fool around with the drinking age, it should start at the other end.

What I mean by this is that the government should first do something about older drinkers before it starts meddling with the younger ones.

There are several reasons I think this:

1. Older people can drink a lot more than younger people because they've had more practice.
2. Also, they can afford more to drink. It's tough to get all that drunk when you're on a six-pack-a-week budget.
3. Older people have a lot more reason to drink than younger people. I drink more now than I did when I was twenty. That's because when I was twenty I hadn't been through three divorces and the Nixon presidency.
4. Older people are sloppier drunks than younger people.

When older people get drunk, they do things like cry, call their ex-wives in Montana and sit around piano bars making fools of themselves trying to sing "Melancholy Baby."

Young people, on the other hand, get sick when they drink too much. A few beers later they throw up and go to bed while their elders are still out crying, calling their ex-wives in Montana and sitting around piano bars making fools of themselves trying to sing "Melancholy Baby."

As we all know by now, the government has blackmailed the states into raising their legal drinking age to twenty-one. Otherwise, the states would face a loss of federal highway funds.

Why Not a Jerk Patrol?

New York City has formed what I presume to be the first bigot patrol in the long history of law enforcement in this country.

The move, announced last week, was instigated after outbreaks of racial violence in the city, "just like down South," as Mayor Ed Koch put it.

Before racial incidents occurred in such places as New York's Howard Beach, Mayor Koch thought bias and prejudice ended just south of Baltimore someplace.

According to reports I read, New York's bigot patrol will work like this:

Cops in plainclothes or disguise will go into neighborhoods

with a history of racial disturbances and act as bait for bigots, or bigot-bait, whichever you prefer.

Black decoys will work Howard Beach, for instance, to deal with anyone manifesting racist tendencies.

Assistant Chief John Holmes, commander of the new unit, explained it all this way:

"We want to say to bigots: the next time you set upon somebody in the streets, he is liable to be a police officer and you are liable to be under arrest."

I hope Archie Bunker has heard about all this.

But why not a bigot patrol? We tried legislation and education as a means of ending prejudice and that hasn't worked. Perhaps a little police muscle will do the trick.

And if the bigot patrol is successful, think of the other social misfits we could round up and haul off in a paddy wagon.

For example, we could have an ugly patrol.

"I'm sorry, sir, but you'll have to come with me downtown."

"But what's the charge, Officer?"

"You're in violation of the city's ugly ordinance. Nobody with a big nose, ears that poke out, or, in your case, is cross-eyed, can be on the streets before dark."

I'd like to see a cliché patrol, too. If there's anything I can't stand it's people who use clichés.

Anybody who says, "Have a nice one," "Hot enough for you?," "So how's the wife?," or "You know" more than five times in any sentence could cool their heels in the slammer for a few days.

I'd get people off the streets whose clothes don't match, too.

"Spread 'em, sucker," a member of the GQ patrol might say, "that tie does not go with that jacket you're wearing. It's vermin like you that give civilization a bad name."

Maybe we could also have a jerk patrol. Think how much better life would be if we didn't have to put up with people who do jerky, annoying things like drive forty in the passing lane, talk loudly in a movie theater, or throw their gum on the sidewalk for some innocent, law-abiding citizen to step on.

People who sneeze as they sit on the stool next to you while you're eating a bowl of soup in a diner, who bring large cassette players onto public conveyances and play music to have a nervous breakdown by, who play slowly on a golf course, who get into the express lane at grocery stores with more than twelve items, who don't put their hand over their heart when the national anthem is being played, who don't use deodorant, have a bad case of dandruff and idiotic ideas you don't agree with.

I don't know why somebody didn't think of using the police to get rid of all our social warts and blemishes before. It's worked in other countries—so why not here?

As Mayor Koch says, "Up against the wall, you redneck mother."

Pollution Without Solution

The environment is supposed to be the main issue of the nineties, and Congress is already hard at work trying to figure out a way to do absolutely nothing about it.

I normally don't get involved in environmental issues, however, because they take too much thought.

It is much easier for me to sit around being concerned about celebrities falling off motorcycles, the spring-training lockout, and whether or not Andy Rooney is a racist.

(I think celebrities who fall off motorcycles deserve it, there are a lot of sportswriters up North who are going berserk because they are not in sunny Florida on expense account, and that Andy Rooney doesn't have a mean bone in his body until he is confronted by a paper clip he doesn't like.)

But if the environment is, indeed, going to be the primary issue of the nineties, I cannot sit idly by writing about much while others are pondering the air we breathe, the water we drink, and whether or not the sun will say the hell with it one morning and not come up.

But if I am going to get into this thing, I want to get into it with both feet.

Sure, I know there's a hole in the ozone layer, tropical rain forests are disappearing, and trees pollute, but have you considered the following:

SECONDHAND ALCOHOL BREATH: If you are on an airplane for instance, and the person next to you is pouring down double scotches, you could get liver damage breathing this person's intoxicating exhales. The solution to this problem is to not allow Ted Kennedy on commercial flights.

POLYESTER POLLUTION: Most people have gotten the word by now that polyester leisure suits are tacky, and they are taking theirs out into the backyard and burning them.

The fumes go into the atmosphere and turn the rain purple, and that's why we are getting such freaks of nature like Prince.

FAT CLOUDS: Everybody is losing weight these days. Where does this weight go? It goes up into the atmosphere, too, and forms big fat clouds, and if you were to be on top of a mountain and walk into one, you could come out with all that weight Oprah Winfrey lost, for instance, and suddenly have a rear end the size of a Buick.

DEPLETION OF THE PULL OF GRAVITY: It's happening. If it weren't, how could Don King's hair stand up straight like that?

THE SILENT SPARROW SYNDROME: If we don't do something to curb those car stereos that blare out music loud enough to be heard in three states, birds are going to quit chirping. What's the use? Who can hear them over 2 Live Crew and their latest repugnant hit?

THE BO-KNOWS-WHERE-IT-BURNS-AND-ITCHES PROBLEM: In the coming years we all will have watched 7 million Bo Jackson commercials on television, and the entire country could develop serious cases of jock itch through some rare form of electrical osmosis.

THE BULL-HOCKEY FACTOR: Scientists say that people who like to hear themselves talk, such as members of Congress, will have uttered approximately 17 septillion trillion pounds of bull-hockey by the year 1995, which can seep into your house through your air-conditioning ducts.

If we don't do something about that, nobody will be saying anything of substance by the turn of the century, and we will all sound like members of Congress talking about the progress of their latest environmental bills out of one side of their mouths while accepting lavish dinner invitations from oil-industry lobbyists out of the other.

I'll Moon You If You Burn Our Flag

I've been thinking about the implications of the recent Supreme Court ruling that says you can burn our flag and go unpunished.

The court ruled any law charging flag-burners with a crime is unconstitutional because the First Amendment protects freedom of speech and expression, no matter how distasteful and disgusting such actions might seem to others.

I can understand some of that. Make a law against burning the flag in protest, and that could lead to a law against burning down a post office in protest of long lines, surly workers, and the fact you just received a nice birthday card from your grandmother, who died in 1962.

Another part of me says, however, that no matter what the Supreme Court ruled, anybody who would burn our flag for any reason is a creep.

But we don't send people to jail just because they're creeps. If we did, our jails would be even more crowded than they already are.

They would be filled with such creepy people as filthy-mouthed rap singers, crooked politicians, and anybody who doesn't realize wrestling is fake—and the Rev. Al Sharpton.

I realize I am really waffling here, but it also seems to me like there ought to be something we could do to flag-burners.

Why do they have to burn our flag, our precious banner of freedom, sacrifice, and history, in the first place?

Couldn't they just burn a photograph of Dan Quayle instead?

I know what we could do to flag-burners instead of sending them to jail. We could send them all back to eleventh-grade American history class, where they would be assigned a term paper on Millard Fillmore.

And it would be due tomorrow. They might at least get a little respect for Old Glory through osmosis.

Regardless, I'd like to see them sweating over Fillmore's stance on the environment.

It also occurred to me—what sort of precedent is this ruling going to set? What other forms of speech and expression come under this ruling?

Can you, in fact, shout "Fire!" in a crowded theater now?

And an even bigger question came to me: "Where does mooning come in here?"

Mooning is a form of expression, isn't it? You drop your drawers at your high school graduation ceremonies and you are expressing the thought "You can all stick it."

Let's say you're in the audience. Do you want the First Amendment tampered with regardless of how distasteful and disgusting it might be to have to look at some zit-faced kid's bare buttocks during "Pomp and Circumstance"?

If we are going to allow people to burn the flag and get away with it, we've got to let them shoot moons, too.

In fact, I'd rather be mooned than see somebody burning the flag. Furthermore, if I ever see somebody burning the flag, I'm going to moon him.

So, be forewarned. It will not be a pretty sight.

Tax 'Em Out on Their Assets

There's a big cry out there to tax the rich. In Congress they scream, "Tax the rich!" They don't mean it, of course, since they're all rich, but it sounds good and might get them reelected so they can come back to Washington and get even richer.

They say President Bush doesn't want to tax the rich. That's because he doesn't know anybody who isn't rich, and that wouldn't be a very nice way to treat your friends.

On the other hand, he could change his mind.

As for me, I certainly think the rich should do their part. But I don't think you can just say, "Tax the rich!"

Not every person who is rich got that way by the same route. The rich should be taxed at rates they deserve, and I have devised my own plan.

I don't think people who got rich because they were smart and thought of a great idea and then busted their tails to make the idea work should be harshly penalized for making a few million honest bucks.

I don't think people who rose from meager beginnings and

worked eighteen hours a day, seven days a week for years until they finally made it should suffer unduly, either.

But there are groups of rich people I think we should stick it to. Send the IRS in with guns and just take what we think we need to help get us out of this financial mess we're in.

You asked for it, and here it is—The Rich People I'd Tax Out of Their Assets:

THE LUCKY-SPERM-CLUB RICH: These are people who just happened to be born in the right place at the right time, the ones who caught the old Fallopian Tube of Fortune.

Daddy did all the work, and now these little snits have the money. If they won't pay, the IRS should cut off the head of one of their polo ponies and put it in the bed with them. It's worked before.

THE ROCK-STAR RICH: They make awful music and still get rich. Then they buy fourteen new cars and mansions with 612 rooms and then decorate each room with tacky furniture.

I'd nail these people, too. Ten percent of their annual earnings for every sofa in their mansions that looks like it once was an animal that lived in or near a jungle.

THE SLIME-BALL RICH: This would include dope and smut dealers, almost everybody currently involved in the film industry (Jessica Tandy being one of the exceptions), anybody who made a lot of money on the polyester hoax that was pulled on the country in the seventies, and the Rev. Al Sharpton. If he doesn't have a lot of money, just take what he has for being loud and obnoxious.

THE COULDN'T-WE-HAVE-DONE-WITHOUT-THEM? RICH: Rich chiropractors.

THE JOCK RICH: Mike Tyson, all boxing promoters, José Canseco, Deion Sanders, and anybody who holds out for 117 days and then signs for $20.5 million and later gives the credit to the Lord for helping him win the game. And George Steinbrenner.

THE ADVERTISING RICH: Find whoever first thought of the phrase "new and improved" and take all his or her money. Also, put a big tax on car dealers who do their own TV commercials, and anybody who has ever done a commercial trying to push insurance off on old people—like Ed McMahon. He's got to be loaded in more ways than one.

THE ELECTED RICH: Find all the people who got rich after being elected to public office. First, tax them. Then, hang them.

Everybody who likes my plan can help by voting against an incumbent every chance they get.

You Gotta Drawer
the Line Somewhere

A report by Knight-Ridder newspapers said it's costing $750 million a day to operate Operation Desert Storm.

Of course, the U.S., which stands for Ultimate Sugar Daddy, is paying for most of it.

It is difficult for me to deal with a notion like $750 million a day. Even "$750 million a month" is bewildering.

I probably could handle "$750 million a decade," because that's what the average baseball player makes these days.

I was further confused by a graphic that accompanied the Knight-Ridder article.

It pictured an American male soldier in full combat gear and what each part of that gear cost. Here're some examples:

- Desert helmet: $103
- Helmet cover: $2.50
- Boots: $33.20
- Socks: $1.65
- M-16 rifle: $475
- Two-quart canteen: $5.45
- Canteen cover: $8.75
- Belt: $6.60
- Suspenders: $6.95

The total estimated cost of outfitting a U.S. soldier came to $1,452.10.

There were a few things in the graphic I had to question.

One is, why does a canteen cover ($8.95) cost more than the canteen itself ($5.45)?

And if we issue a soldier a belt ($6.60), why does he also need suspenders ($6.95)?

The thing that concerned me most, however, was what we're paying for a soldier's drawers.

Out of the $1,412.10 being spent on the combat outfit, a measly $1.50 is spent on a soldier's underwear.

Have you priced men's drawers lately? Put a "Calvin Klein" or

"Ralph Lauren" tag on them and they cost you twenty bucks or more.

Nondesigner drawers cost anywhere from ten to eighteen bucks.

And the ones we're giving our soldiers cost only a dollar-fifty?

There's nothing worse than a cheap pair of drawers. Wear them a couple of times and the elastic waistband stretches and suddenly you're wearing a most annoying and uncomfortable piece of clothing, commonly known as "droopy drawers."

It's tough just going to work in droopy drawers.

Ten times a day they fall down from the waist to just north of the knees. You have to go to the men's room, take off your pants, and pull up your drawers.

This causes the loss of valuable time in the workplace, not to mention considerable irritability.

Imagine how it would be to try and fight a war while wearing droopy drawers.

You can't just stop in the desert, pull down your desert trousers ($14.40), and pull up your droopy drawers.

I couldn't locate a military expert, retired or otherwise, to speak on this subject. They were all tied up with the networks.

But I think it is a damnable shame we don't think enough of our boys on the battlefront to give them a proper, functional pair of drawers.

It's just like our government to go hog-wild on canteen covers and suspenders, but basically ignore a much more important item—underwear.

I don't know what we can do here at home unless it's this: If you've got a man in the desert, send him some drawers.

Even if you can't afford Calvins or Ralphs, there are many

more less-expensive fruits of the looms available, and they won't become droopy.

Operation Desert Drawers. It's time to act.

Gulf War Notes

Closing the notebook of the War in the Gulf; a farewell to arms.

SCHWARZKOPF FOR PRESIDENT: We haven't had a military person in the White House since Ike. How could anybody not vote for the man who won the War in the Gulf, Stormin' Norman?

Only one way: if he ran as a Democrat.

BEER: American troops had to do without for months as they served in Saudi Abstentia. Here's a great public-service idea:

Why don't the big brewers give each returning soldier all the brew he or she can drink for a year? Call your local distributors with this patriotic suggestion.

MISFIRE: The term from the war with the best chance of remaining a part of our language: "Scud."

SUGGESTED NEXT ASSIGNMENT FOR PETER ARNETT: Stationed inside the IRS as it decides who to audit.

SUGGESTED PUNISHMENT FOR SADDAM HUSSEIN IN HELL:
Bury his head in the camel dung pit for the first ten thousand
years; then put him in the Rat, Snake, Spider, and Scorpion
Room next to the ayatollah.

SWEET SURRENDER: After hearing Iraqi soldiers had surren-
dered to an Italian news photographer, a guy said, "That's the
first time in history the Italians have taken a prisoner of war."

SUGGESTED NEXT ASSIGNMENT FOR WOLF BLITZER: Anything that gets him away from reporting from in front of the
same map for two months.

**DAN QUAYLE'S TOP THREE CONTRIBUTIONS
TO THE WAR EFFORT:**
(1) He learned to dress himself every morning during the cri-
     sis, allowing Marlin Fitzwater more time to work on press
     briefings.
(2) He stuck to the script prepared for him in speeches and
     didn't say one single incredibly stupid thing.
(3) He stayed up to watch *Nightline* twice.

GOOD POINT: A mother wrote a newspaper suggesting another condition Iraq should be made to accept is changing the
spelling of its country.

"I've tried to teach my children a 'q' is always followed by a
'u,' " she wrote. "They watch war reports on television and tell
me I'm wrong."

THAT'S WHAT I WOULD HAVE DONE: Reports said Iraqi soldiers broke into a Kuwait City communications center and
hauled out a load of computers they thought were televisions.
When they discovered they weren't, they smashed the screens.

BEST CLEAN JOKE OF THE WAR: Quickest way to break up an Iraqi bingo game? Call B-52.

BEST DIRTY JOKE OF THE WAR: Has to do with an Iraqi with a pig under one arm and a sheep under the other. Use your imagination.

BEST PRESIDENT IN OFFICE DURING A WAR SINCE FDR: Big George.

BEST HEADLINE I SAW DURING THE WAR: UNLEASHED, from the *Sunday Atlanta Journal and Constitution*, announcing the start of the ground campaign.

BEST WORD TO APPEAR IN ANY WAR HEADLINE: PEACE.

10 SPORTS

The Wide World of Us Versus Them

Pulling the Wool
Over My Eyes

I found my old high school letter jacket the other day. I was looking for something else in the back of a closet at my mother's house and came upon it—blue with off-white leather sleeves and a block N sewn on the front.

I had forgotten it even existed. I suppose that twenty-four years ago when I graduated from high school, I simply cast it aside as I leaped into the more material collegiate world.

"I put it up for you and kept it," my mother said, "in case you ever wanted it again."

I played basketball and baseball at Newnan High School. I lettered in both sports, which is how I got the jacket in the first place. My number, 12, is stitched on one of the sleeves. The face of a tiger—our mascot—is on the other.

Enough years have passed now that I probably could lie about my high school athletic career and get away with most of it.

I know guys who barely made the varsity who've managed to move up to all-state status with the passing of enough years.

But I'll be honest. I was an average athlete, if that. I averaged maybe ten points a game in basketball, and shot the thing on every opportunity that came to me.

"Grizzard is the only person who never had a single assist in his entire basketball career," an ex-teammate was telling some-one in my presence. "That's because he never passed the ball."

I hit over .300 my senior year in baseball, but they were all bloop singles except for one of those bloopers that rolled in some high weeds in right field. By the time the ball was found, I was around the bases for the winning run.

"Why don't you take it home with you?" my mother sug-gested after I had pulled the jacket out of the closet. "Maybe you'll have some children one day and they might like to see it."

I reminded my mother I was forty-one and down three mar-riages, and the future didn't look that bright for offspring. But I suppose a mother can dream.

I did bring the jacket home with me. Alone, up in my bed-room, in front of a mirror, I pulled it over me for the first time in a long time.

A lot of names came back with the jacket. Clay, John, Buddy, Russell, Richard, Al. And Dudley and the Hound, who's still looking for his first base hit since he was fifteen.

And then there was Wingo, of course, the best high school shortstop I ever saw until a ground ball hit a pebble one day and bounced up and broke his jaw.

Ever hear that haunting song "Where Are the Men I Used to Sport With?"

They've all got kids, I guess, and their mothers are happy.

It's funny about my jacket. It still fit well on my arms and shoulders, but I couldn't get it to button anymore.

I guess some shrinkage can be expected after all those years of neglect in the closet.

Risking My Life
for a Good War

I was walking behind a friend and his wife as we entered the Superdome in New Orleans on January 1, 1981, to watch Georgia play Notre Dame in the Sugar Bowl. If Georgia won, the Bulldogs would be the 1980 national collegiate football champions.

My friend, a fellow Georgia alumnus, was fraught with anticipation. He was pale. He was nervous. He was perspiring profusely. No, he wasn't. He was sweating like a Clemson fan trying to write a love letter.

His wife, noticing his condition, said, "Calm down, sweetheart. It's just a football game."

He stopped dead. He turned to his wife, who had not gone to Georgia—and went to Bulldog games with her husband simply because she thought it was her wifely duty—looked her squarely in the eyes and said:

"It is not just a football game. It's our way of life against theirs."

He meant that. I knew the man well enough to know he did, in fact, mean that.

It had something to do with Southerners against Northerners. Maybe it even had something to do with his Methodist upbringing and the pope.

Whatever, it was clearly Us versus Them. Us won that day: tailback Herschel Walker leading Georgia to the national title.

After the game, the cry on Bourbon Street into the wee hours was "Us versus Them" again, as in: "Y'all got the hunchback. We got the tailback."

You can go into all that stuff about the pageantry of college football, the fact the players are unspoiled kids and not a bunch of millionaires and it's a nice way to spend an afternoon with friends.

But with me and mine, and, with a lot of others, college football offers us an opportunity to circle our wagons and fight and kick and scream for our side against their side.

College football and allegiances are clear as an October Saturday afternoon. It's so simple: I want anything wearing red and black to tear the head off anything that isn't.

We haven't had a good war in over fifty years, one that wasn't all tangled up in dissent and questionable motives. For all I know, George Bush was, in fact, more concerned about oil than he was about the people of Kuwait when he ordered Operation Desert Storm to commence.

But when Georgia meets Florida in the Gator Bowl, when Auburn plays Alabama, when Ohio State goes against Michigan, there are no such nagging annoyances.

We were right and we knew we were right to wipe away the Nazi scourge and the Japanese militarists in World War II. And in the case of Georgia fans, we know we are right to want to beat Florida.

Our way of life against theirs. Clear as a bell.

Congress can waste your money, the president can lie to you, and your kid can wear an earring and watch MTV, but if your alma mater is 8–0, who's sweating the small stuff?

I once risked my life because of college football.

In late August of 1985, I found myself in a hospital in London with a deadly infection of the artificial aortic valve in my heart. The British doctor said it would probably be necessary for me to remain there for six weeks' treatment.

Georgia was to open its 1985 football season on Labor Day night against Alabama in Athens. I slipped out of the hospital, caught a cab to Gatwick Airport and flew back to Atlanta.

When asked later why I would risk my life in such a manner, I said, I wasn't about to stay in no foreign country during college football season.

Us could win them all in '93, by the way, or Us could lose a few. But, right or wrong, win or lose, always Us.

Making Athletes Study

Sooner or later, I knew a bunch of schoolteachers would decide athletes had to study and become educated like the other students.

This, of course, is what has happened in Texas—of all places—where the "no-pass, no-play" rule has gone into effect. Other states, I am certain, soon will follow Texas's lead.

I don't think we have thought this thing out. As a matter of fact, I believe we may be making a terrible mistake in insisting schoolboy athletes become educated.

There are several reasons I believe this:

1. Students who aren't athletes have enough trouble as it is. I mean, how many dates can you get off your annual Science Club project?

About all these students had to look forward to was the future, when, because of their superior grades, they could expect to get all the good jobs with IBM while all the dumb jocks would end up working at dumb jobs.

If we insist athletes learn while in school, then the other students not only won't have dates, but they also probably will lose out when the IBM jobs are up for grabs.

Let's face it. If both applicants have the same grades, who is IBM going to pick, a former all-state quarterback or some wimp?

2. If we start educating athletes, we could wind up with a lot more politicians like Jack Kemp.

3. How many athletes are going to continue to play such games as football if we teach them to think for themselves?

Football is a fun game to watch, but it really can't be that much fun to play. You run around out there and large people are trying to knock you down to the ground.

Football players have to learn such uncomfortable tactics as "playing hurt," and "sucking it up." Plus, you can get a variety of rashes and diseases hanging out in locker rooms.

What intelligent person is going, as the coaches say, "to pay the price?"

Educate our athletes and most of them will quit playing ball and start hanging around playing video games with the other students.

4. Give an athlete a quality education and he might start saying intelligent things to the media. As it is, the media can sim-

ply make up quotes for athletes because they always say the same things.

"Well, you know, Skip, you know, God gave me, you know, the talent, you know, to play this game, you know, and if you, you know, need any more information, you know, you know you can, you know, get in touch, you know, with my agent."

5. And speaking of the media, if we quit turning out dumb jocks, where will our TV color come from?

6. Educate today's athletes, and today's coaches, yesterday's jocks, will not be able to communicate with their players anymore.

COACH: "Willoughby, what were you thinking about when you made that play?"
WILLOUGHBY: "Goethe."

7. If "no-pass, no-play" spreads, there won't be any more dumb-jock jokes like the one where the teacher asks an offensive guard how many seconds there are in a year, and after some contemplation, he answers: "There are twelve. January second, February second, et cetera."

8. And think of this: If athletes become smart, they will stop accepting the charges when the president calls their locker rooms to congratulate them.

Pig Polo

PALM BEACH, FLORIDA—Here at the playground of the rich in south Florida, you can pick up a newspaper and find reports from the polo matches on the front page of the sports section where baseball ought to be.

Obviously, polo is very important to the well-heeled of the area who drive out to the matches in their Rollses and then discuss between chukkers how difficult it is to find good help these days.

I have never seen a polo match and neither has anyone I know. A friend of mine, Glenn McCutchen, says he was in Palm Beach on business once and actually attempted to see a little polo.

"I read there was going to be a match at the Palm Beach Polo Club," Glenn reported, "and so I asked somebody at the front desk at my hotel how to get there.

"He looked over at me, turned up his nose and said, 'I'm sorry, sir, but I am not allowed to divulge such information to anyone from the masses.'"

I didn't make it to the polo matches during my stay in Palm Beach, either. When I asked at my hotel for directions to the club, the man behind the desk suggested I go bowling instead.

I was quite discouraged, because the reason I wanted to see a polo match in the first place involved a humanitarian effort on behalf of America's beleaguered farmers.

This all began when I received a letter some time ago from one David S. Burre, who has an engineering firm in Atlanta.

Mr. Burre pointed out that he and a group of his friends were drinking one evening in a place called the High Horse Tavern and came up with a way for farmers to get out of their financial straits.

The idea goes something like this: In every small town and village in America, there should be established a polo franchise.

Because polo ponies are so expensive, Mr. Burre's idea is to have the game played while mounted on pigs.

"Pig polo," said David Burre. "Finally the layman, for a small investment of three hundred and fifty dollars, could own a thoroughbred-type animal—a polo pig—and think of the money farmers could make selling pigs to pig polo franchises.

Mr. Burre and his friends, who admittedly birthed his idea after a night of considerable consumption, already have devised rules for pig polo. Here are a few:

- A period is called a "lard."
- No slopping of the pigs between lards.
- No rooting, for the home team or otherwise, allowed.
- Umpires are licensed USDA inspectors.

I think this idea has merit. It's time we helped the farmer and it's time the rest of us—members of the great unwashed—were given the opportunity to enjoy the great sport of polo, even if we have to ride pigs to do it.

I don't know what the spiffy types in Palm Beach do after a

polo match is over, but in David Burre's pig polo, the fun has just begun when the final oink is sounded.

In pig polo, you see, the winners get to celebrate by cooking and eating the losers' mounts.

My Most Valuable Players

I was having an impromptu interview with Howard Fox, a member of the executive committee of the Minnesota Twins baseball team, during a Twins spring training game against the world-champion New York Mets, a group of famous millionaires.

Mr. Fox told me something I didn't know. He said the average salary for major-league baseball players today is in excess of $400,000 a year.

That's the *average* salary.

"How do these guys get paid," I asked, "by the week?"

"Twice a month, but just during the season," he answered.

"Do you mail their checks to their banks, or to their agents?" I continued.

"Most of our guys come by and we hand them their checks," said Mr. Fox.

I did some figuring. Let's say a player makes $1 million a year, which a lot of them do, even utility infielders.

He's paid twice weekly for approximately six months, so that means each time he's handed his check his gross is for something around $83,000.

I'm for everybody making all the bucks he or she can, but every time I watch a bunch of spoiled crybaby baseball players, like the Mets, it makes me even more aware of how we need to reward others in our society with a lot more than they are making.

I made a list of some examples:

SCHOOLTEACHERS: If it weren't for my teachers, I couldn't have figured out the biweekly check for a millionaire ballplayer.

My mother taught first grade for thirty years. The first six months of every year, she worked mostly on housebreaking half her class. She went back to teaching in 1953 after she and my father divorced. She was paid $120 a month. Batboys make more than that.

AIRLINE PILOTS: They already make a lot of money, but they also should have a bonus clause that says each time they land one of those tubs safely, they get a few more bucks.

I want my airline pilots to have a great deal of incentive to get me back on the ground safely.

COPS AND FIREMEN: Next time you're getting mugged or your house is on fire, call your favorite utility infielder.

SECRETARIES: Most executives could not function were it not for their secretaries. Relief pitchers in baseball are paid according to how many "saves" they have.

Secretaries should be paid on the same basis for the number of times they save their bosses from embarrassing situations, such as being discovered as total incompetents.

GARBAGEMEN: They keep us from being overrun by our own wastefulness, and for a paltry pittance of pay we expect them to take away our garbage at five in the morning and not make any noise.

MINISTERS WHO DON'T HAVE THEIR OWN TV SHOWS: These are the people who don't make very much money, yet they still console the troubled, visit the sick, and pray for the dead, and don't get to wear any makeup.

Jim Bakker, Jerry Falwell, Jimmy Swaggart, et al., couldn't carry their Bibles.

Think about it. And the next time you need somebody to lean on, call Darryl Strawberry.

Oh, Deer, the Hunt Is On

Deer hunting season began Saturday. According to an article I read, there'll be more guys with guns in the woods in my environs just Saturday than there are American troops in Saudi Arabia.

I'll sleep well tonight knowing I'm not only safe from Saddam Hussein, but from the ferocious deer as well.

There was some other deer news in the papers. A jury in Maine brought back an Innocent verdict against a deer hunter charged with manslaughter.

He's out in the woods of Maine and he sees something white, so he takes a couple of shots.

What he saw was a young mother of infant twins, who was in her backyard wearing white mittens. She died from the gunshots.

In her backyard!

A portion of the hunter's defense, I read, was that the dead woman wasn't a native of Maine and didn't know about all the hunting that went on and should not have been in her backyard wearing white mittens.

I'm really not against deer hunting, per se, but I've said all along it could be a much fairer sport (if killing anything can be called a sport) if they would just change some of the rules of the game.

So I have put some great thought into this, and can now offer you Grizzard's Revised Rules of Hunting Down Deer and Blowing Them Away:

RULE NO. 1: If you kill a deer, you have to eat it. None of this trophy killing or shooting a deer for the sheer thrill of seeing it fall.

We kill cows so that we can have hamburger, so killing a deer in order to have something good to eat, I think, is okay.

An addendum to Rule No. 1 is you have to eat the entire deer if you kill it. Okay, you don't have to eat the pancreas or the large intestines, but whatever's edible, you've got to eat it all.

Addendum No. 2 to Rule No. 1 is you can't kill a second deer until you've eaten all your first one.

If you kill a second deer, a game warden will be sent to your house to check out your freezer and make certain there was none of the first deer left.

If you kill a second deer before you eat all the first one, you have to eat the pancreas of the second one, but you can prepare it any way you wish. I am a fair man.

RULE NO. 2: You have to hunt in the nude. The deer aren't dressed, are they? All that camouflage is nothing but trickery, and should not be allowed if this thing is to be truly fair. I realize you might get a little nippy out there, and there's all those briers and barbed-wire fences, but, hey, this ain't no Easter egg hunt.

RULE NO. 3: Forget Uzis and bazookas. You can have only one bullet when you go hunting.

Barney had only one bullet and Andy didn't even carry a gun, and they kept Mayberry safe. Sorry, pal, you missed. Go home and get another bullet and you can try tomorrow.

RULE NO. 4: If you do happen to shoot another person by mistake, it would be quite tacky to ask the family of the departed to allow you to have the head of the victim to put on the wall in the den. Except in Maine, where it's sort of expected.

RULE NO. 5: You cannot at any time say you hunt deer because you (1) are doing the deer a favor by killing them because if you don't, there'll be too many deer and a lot of them will starve; or (2) it's your way of communing with nature.

If you're worried about the deer starving, why not take some food into the woods and feed the poor things instead of killing them?

And if all you want to do is commune with nature, get a pair of binoculars and go watch birds. That way if you spot a red-headed, three-toed, black-billed ratbird, there are no rules you have to eat the darn thing, as there are in deer hunting.

RULE NO. 6: If you do not follow Rules 1 through 5, the next time you're in the woods, may Smokey the Bear eat you for your hat, which is what he's been doing to Boy Scouts for years.

Why I Get No Kick Out of Soccer

Twenty-one reasons why I hate soccer and wouldn't pay attention to a World Cup match if it was going on in my backyard and the beer was free:

1. There are only three final scores in soccer. They are 0–0, 1–0, and in a real scoring orgy, 1–1.
2. Being able to bounce a ball off one's head isn't that impressive to me. I've seen countless seals do the same thing on *The Ed Sullivan Show.*
3. Soccer breeds fan violence because it's very dull, and when the fans get bored, they pass the time by trying to kill and maim one another.
4. Nobody ever throws a high, inside fastball in soccer, baseball's answer to killing and maiming.
5. A man named Phil Woosnam, then president of the North American Soccer League, once bragged to me, "In twenty years, soccer will be bigger than pro football in the United States." That was twenty-five years ago.

6. Soccer is responsible for soccer-style kickers in American football. I agree with the late Norman Van Brocklin, who was asked his reaction to the game, after his Atlanta Falcons had been beaten on a last-minute field goal by some guy from Yugoslavia or Afghanistan.

   Van Brocklin said, "They ought to tighten the immigration laws in this country."

7. It was a referee's controversial call in a soccer match that started World War I.

   No, I can't prove that, but I don't have to.

8. Too many soccer teams wear dark socks with their shorts, a violation of every fashion law ever written.

9. The theme song for the British Broadcasting Corporation's coverage of the World Cup is Luciano Pavarotti's version of "Nessun Dorma," from Puccini's opera *Turandot*.

   The theme song of WGN's coverage of the Chicago Cubs baseball is Harry Caray singing "Take Me Out to the Ball Game."

10. If soccer were an American politician, it would be Alan Cranston.

11. If it were an American actress, it would be Florence Henderson.

12. Parents of kids who play soccer in American schools are overbearing and obnoxious. It's because they are secretly upset their kids were too wormy to try out for football.

13. My alma mater, the University of Georgia, overcame all sorts of odds and won the College Baseball World Series. I realize that doesn't have a thing to do with soccer, but I just thought I would mention it.

14. If Georgia has a soccer team, I am blissfully unaware of it.

15. Bo doesn't know diddly about soccer.

. was in London once and watched the Super Bowl of British soccer matches on television because there wasn't anything else on. The two teams ran up and down the field for approximately three hours, but nobody could score.

They decided to play another game two nights later. I watched that, too. I'd seen all the churches, museums, and china shops I wanted to see by that time.

They ran up and down the field again for an hour or two, and then the ball hit a player in the head and went into the goal completely by accident, and the final score was 1–0. When the game was over, two guys came on the screen and analyzed it for forty-five minutes.

17. If soccer were a vegetable, it would be asparagus.
18. Hitler was probably a soccer fan.
19. Parents of American children who play soccer will react violently to number 12 and write me a lot of nasty, threatening letters. Hey, it's what they deserve for raising wimps.
20. If soccer were an American soft drink, it would be Diet Pepsi.
21. How 'bout them Dawgs?

For Sale: One Complete Ski Outfit

I used to go skiing about this time each year, despite the fact that natives of the Deep South know their way around snow much the same as a rhinoceros knows its way around roller skates.

It used to cost me quite a bit of money to go skiing. After buying ski pants and ski socks and ski jackets and ski sweaters and ski underwear, I still had to buy a plane ticket that would fly me two thousand miles to some expensive ski resort out West.

Then I had to rent skis and boots and buy lift tickets.

All this to have the opportunity to stand atop a mountain in subzero temperatures trembling in fear as I tried to figure out how I could get to the bottom to thaw out without killing or maiming myself, not to mention what might happen to others who came into my path.

It would have been simpler, and cheaper, to have gotten a root canal. I could have had the same amount of fun.

The reason I began skiing in the first place is I am gullible.

My friend said, "Why don't you go skiing with me? You'll love it."

I believed him. I really believed I would go skiing and fall in love with it, and become a great skier and change my name to Lars Earl. (You know how Southerners like double first names.)

I didn't love skiing after I tried it once, but I have continued to ski because I thought it would get easier and more comfortable.

Wrong again. The hassle factor in the sport of skiing never eased for me.

First there were the boots. Ski boots weigh approximately the same as a Honda.

It takes the better part of an hour to get them on because

of the number of straps and buckles that have to be fastened.

Walking in a pair of ski boots is another matter. The next time you watch *Cool Hand Luke*, notice how easily the prisoners move with a ball and chain and you will know what it is like to attempt to walk in a pair of ski boots.

Then comes the lift, which is what you ride to the top of the mountain in order to ski back down it.

There is always a long line waiting on the lift. And I always got on with somebody who weighed six hundred pounds and made the lift chair lean dangerously.

Once I tried to get off a lift with a four-hundred-pound ski bunny sitting next to me. She fell during her dismount and landed on top of me.

Big Foot lives.

Skiing can be embarrassing, too. I never fell when I was skiing alone or when I was off on some distant run. I always fell either in the lift line or directly under the lift, so I always had an audience, which inevitably included small children, from places like Utah and Colorado, who would point and laugh at me.

All this to say I'm not going to return to the slopes as usual this winter. As a matter of fact, I'm never going skiing again.

The bother isn't worth it. And snow ain't my style.

Ol' Lars Earl here has hung up his boots for good.

See you where the sun shines.

11 THE SOUTH

"You Bubbas Are All Alike"

Song of the Lower East

The South continues to have a terrible public relations problem.

I became aware of this at the Super Bowl that was held in Atlanta last month. The city, which is in the South, was even ripped by a Chicago columnist.

That doesn't concern me greatly because I know there's never much Super Bowl news for sportswriters, so the way to get one day behind you is to write a column knocking whatever city you happen to be visiting on expense account.

It's a cliché, but it beats writing about large linemen.

It's a little odd that somebody who lives in Chicago would have the guts to rip Sioux City, much less Atlanta.

But Atlanta is in the South, so it's easy to throw in a few "sho' nuff"'s and "kiss my grits"'s and a mention or two of molasses, which, of course, is what we put on our grits.

It was the controversy over Georgia's state flag that really pointed to the PR problem. The Georgia state flag includes a replica of the Confederate flag, and many felt it was inappropriate for a symbol of the Civil War to be shown at the Super Bowl. There were televised protests.

The Civil War, of course, was the war between the North and

the South, which the North won by two touchdowns after the South had kept it fairly close for a half.

It also involved the issue of the enslavement of black people, which was taking place in the South at the time. Quite naturally then, many people, including the Rev. Jesse Jackson, are against the public display of any symbol that allegedly glorifies the South's stance in those days, the state flag being just one of them.

I have also heard the same thing mentioned about the carvings of Confederates Robert E. Lee and his fellow generals on Atlanta's Stone Mountain, and all those Confederate monuments on all the squares in small towns throughout Georgia and the South.

But here's the problem: We can change the state flag. We can chisel off Lee and we can tear down Confederate monuments. We got rid of the song "Dixie," didn't we?

But this portion of the United States will still be known as "the South," as in "the South that rebelled against the rest of the country," "the South, where people eat and talk funny" and "the South, which once fought a war to keep its slaves."

As long as we're known as the South, we've got that serious PR problem.

Today I propose a solution—a new name for the region. As soon as we rid ourselves of every symbol of the Civil War, as soon as we lose our accents, as soon as we stop eating molasses and grits, then we start calling ourselves something other than the South, which has so many negative connotations.

I suggest we call ourselves "the Lower East."

It has a nice ring to it, doesn't it?

And we are, in fact, located in the lower eastern part of the

United States. By calling ourselves the Lower East, we would be both politically and geographically correct.

Actually, when we're asked or mocked in the North with "Well, sho' nuff, honey chile, where are you all from?" we can answer, "We all is from L.E."

We could talk about Lower Eastern hospitality and Good Ol' Lower Eastern cooking and if we could ever convince Ted Turner to stop showing *Gone With the Wind* on the Super Station, perhaps in time everybody would forget there ever was a South, a Civil War, hoop skirts, and all that stuff.

And we don't have earthquakes in L.E.

Sho' nuff?

Sure enough.

This is going to be easier than I thought.

Southerners Learning Not to Speak Southern

There have been several reports recently of Southerners going to special classes in an effort to learn not to speak Southern.

I read of such classes in Atlanta, where people who took the course said they were afraid if they didn't stop talking with a Southern accent, it might impede their progress toward success.

A young woman who works for IBM said, "I want to advance through the company and I feel I need to improve my voice. . . ."

What she really was saying is the IBM office where she works is run by a bunch of northern transplants who probably make fun of the way she talks, and she is embarrassed and wants to talk like they do.

That, in my opinion, is grounds for loss of Southern citizenship.

What are we trying to do here? Do we all want to sound like those talking heads on local television news who have tried so hard not to have an accent, their vocal cords are nervous wrecks?

What's wrong with having a Southern accent? My grandfather said "y'all" (only in the plural sense, however, as Yankees have never figured out) and my grandmother said, "I reckon." And if IBM doesn't like that kind of talk, they can just program themselves right back to where they came from.

I like accents. I like to try to emulate accents, other than my own.

I do a big-time Texas oilman: "Now, you ladyfolks just run along 'cause us menfolk got to talk about bidness."

I can even talk—or at least type—like Bostonians sound: "Where can I pock my cah?"

The wonderful thing about the way Americans treat the English language is we have sort of made it up as we have gone along, and I see absolutely nothing wrong with having different ways to pronounce different words.

New Yorkers say "mudder and fadder."

Midwesterners say "mahmee and dee-ad."

Southerners say "mahma and deadie."

Big deal.

If we all spoke the same, dressed the same, acted the same,

thought the same, then this country would not be the unique place that it is, would not have the benefit of our spice and variety, and everybody probably would be in the Rotary Club.

What we all need to realize is the more diverse we are, the stronger we are. Being able to get second and third and even fourth and fifth opinions often will prevent the nastiest of screw-ups.

I say if you are going to classes to lose your Southern accent, you are turning your back on your heritage, and I hope you wind up working behind the counter of a convenience store with three Iranians and a former Indian holy man.

And if you happen to be from another part of the country and make fun of the way Southerners talk, may you be elected permanent program chairman of your Rotary Club.

Y'all reckon I've made my point?

Resolutions, Southern Style

I can pride myself on two major accomplishments in 1990. Both have to do with my fondness for down-home Southern cooking.

I favor down-home Southern cooking because I am from a down-home Southern home. That, and it tastes good.

I want my chicken fried, my steak with gravy, my green beans cooked, and my tomatoes served raw.

Too many fancy restaurants serve their green beans raw and then they cook their tomatoes—and give you some sort of hard, dark bread with it. This is an unholy aberration I cannot abide.

I find the best down-home Southern cooking at a small restaurant in Atlanta, which features fried chicken, country-fried steak, meat loaf, and, on Fridays, beef tips on rice and home-cooked vegetables—and uncooked tomatoes, of course.

Imagine my shock, however, when I went to order my vegetables one day and the list on the menu included "Northern beans."

"There must be some mistake," I said to my favorite waitress, Jo. "This says, 'Northern beans.' How can you list Northern beans in a down-home Southern cooking place?"

"What do you call them?" asked Jo.

" 'White soup beans,' of course," I answered.

My mother used to cook white soup beans for me.

It's a little-known fact, but when Jesus fed the masses, he served white soup beans with the fish and bread. "Northern beans" aren't mentioned anywhere in the Bible.

Jo said, "I'll see what I can do."

I come in a week later, and it says "White soup beans" on the menu. Praise Him.

Accomplishment No. 1.

Another place I often eat is at a golf club in Atlanta, which has good chili.

Chili is down-home as long as you don't put any mushrooms in it. They serve corn bread with the down-home chili at the club.

The problem is, the corn bread is sweet. Corn bread is not supposed to be sweet. That's in the Bible, too. The Book of Martha White, 7:11.

If you want something sweet, order the pound cake. Anybody who puts sugar in the corn bread is a heathen who doesn't love the Lord, not to mention Southeastern Conference football.

Anyway, in late December I went to the club and ordered the chili.

"You ought to try the corn bread," said the waiter. "The chef got tired of you complaining, so he quit putting sugar in it."

I tasted the corn bread. No sugar. I called out the chef.

"Verily," I said unto him, "it's about time you stopped making a sacrilege out of corn bread."

Accomplishment No. 2.

I feel so good about my two feats of 1990, I've got two new targets for '91.

I'm going to see if I can convince fast-food places to start cutting up their own french fries instead of using frozen ones, and I'm going to see if I can help white bread make a comeback in this country.

Do not underestimate me. I'm on a mission from God.

Life Span in Georgia

A recent study of the life spans of men and women showed that Georgia is near the bottom in a ranking of states.

Hawaii and Minnesota were the states where people live the longest.

Hawaii, of course, features a warm tropical climate where people sit around drinking various exotic concoctions made with pineapple juice and watch lovely young girls in grass skirts move their sensuous bodies to ukulele music.

The only drawback to living a long time in Hawaii is you get very old and your eyesight eventually goes, so you can no longer see the young girls move their bodies, but you still have to put up with all that ukulele music.

As to Minnesota, nobody really lives a long time there. It's so cold it just seems like it.

Being a Georgian, I naturally was concerned upon discovering I can't expect to live as long as people from other states.

Georgia is a marvelously diverse state, with mountains and seashores and charming small towns and, of course, bustling exciting Atlanta.

So what makes us die earlier than other Americans? I put some thought to this question and came up with the following:

ATLANTA TRAFFIC: Other cities have traffic jams; Atlanta has traffic wars. General Sherman burned this city. The highway department is dismantling it, piece by piece.

There is so much highway construction in Atlanta, motorists have to wear hard hats. Rather than face another day in Atlanta traffic, a lot of people simply die to avoid it.

GNATS: Gnats, tiny bugs, are the cause of a number of deaths in south Georgia each year. Some of these deaths have been attributed to swallowing a large number of gnats while talking or eating.

Some also think the reason a lot of south Georgians disappear and never are heard from again is they are carried off by giant swarms of gnats and drowned in the Okefenokee Swamp.

KUDZU: Nothing grows faster than a kudzu vine. It has been known to cover entire homes in Georgia while the families are asleep for the night. They are then trapped inside and can't get to a convenience store, so they starve.

Those who try to eat their way out of kudzu quickly have their innards entangled in the vine, because no matter how much you chew it, the blamed stuff just keeps on growing.

THE FALCONS: The Falcons lost a game to the Chicago Bears, 36–0, and the Falcons' coach blamed it on poor officiating. The Falcons have been big losers most every year they've been in Atlanta. A man fell out of the stadium during a Falcons game once and was killed. I think he jumped after another Falcons holding penalty.

LIVING IN BUCKHEAD: Buckhead is a tiny section of Atlanta, similar to those in other large metropolitan areas, where about eleven million white people under the age of thirty-five live.

Each evening, all eleven million get into their Mercedeses and go to trendy Buckhead bars and talk to one another. Here is what a Buckhead bar conversation usually sounds like:

"I was like, 'Wow!' and he was like, 'Really?' "

These people might die from wearing their designer jeans too tight, choking on hearts of palm while eating their salads or being trampled by a polo pony.

The study further revealed at what time of year most Georgians die. It's when the state legislature is in session.

The "Bubba" Stereotype

For years I have attempted to enlighten those individuals who hold biased and ill-based opinions about the name "Bubba."

Most think men named Bubba are nothing more than ignorant swine who wear caps with the names of heavy-equipment dealers on the front, shoot anything that moves, listen to music about doing bodily harm to hippies, and put beer on their grits.

There may be Bubbas who fit the above description, but there are plenty who don't.

Earlier, I wrote of a man—college educated, with no tobacco-juice stains on his teeth—whose family had always referred to him as Bubba.

"I got that name," he explained, "because my baby sister couldn't say brother. She called me Bubba."

The man's problem was that he had taken a job with some sort of high-tech corporation, and his boss insisted he drop the name Bubba because he felt clients wouldn't respect a man with such a name.

Our Bubba refused to use any other name, however, and became quite successful with his new company and wound up with his former boss's job. The former boss now refers to his old employee as "Mr. Bubba."

Anyway, I happened to pick up a back issue of *Southerner* magazine recently, and on the very front cover were the following words:

"Bubba! You don't have to be dumb, mean, fat, slow, white or male to be one!"

I turned to page 37 and began to read:

"Of all the Southern stereotypes," the story began, "the one that answers to 'Bubba' is probably the least flattering."

The article went on to do portraits of eight Bubbas. Do any of the following fit the typical "Bubba" stereotype?

- *Keith (Bubba) Taniguchi:* Attorney, Austin, Texas. Full-blooded Japanese. Into Zen.
- *John (Bubba) Trotman:* State director of the USDA's Agricultural Stabilization and Conservation Service, Montgomery, Alabama. On people moving into Alabama: "At first, they say, 'Alabama, that's Tobacco Road. Then, you can't blow them out of Alabama with a cannon.' "
- *Efula (Bubba) Johnson:* Narcotics officer, Savannah, Georgia. Mr. Johnson is a large black man, and he carries a large gun.
- *Walter (Bubba) Smith:* Minister, Ashdown, Arkansas. Claims no relation to Bubba Smith of football and beer commercial fame.
- *James (Bubba) Armstrong:* Surgeon, Montgomery, Alabama. Careful poking fun at anybody who knows his way around a scalpel.
- *Paula (Bubba) Meiner:* Owns a barbecue joint in Winter Park, Florida. Nice lady.

- *Bernard (Bubba) Meng, III:* State administrator for U.S. Senator Ernest Hollings, Columbia, South Carolina. He's "Little Bubba." Dad was "Big," etc.
- *Kyle (Bubba) Patrick:* Elementary school student, Auburntown, Tennessee. He wants to be a basketball player when he grows up.

One more thing: The University of Georgia veterinary school recently produced the state's first test-tube calf, a Holstein bull weighing one hundred pounds.

They named him Bubba. What else?

A Vote in Favor of Bubba

When the 1992 presidential primaries moved South, the media was full of references to "the Bubba vote."

Yet, when the primaries were in the East, nobody referred to "the loud-talking Yankee vote." When they went to the Midwest, there was no mention of "the frozen fools vote." When it was time for the California primary, there was nothing said about "the nut and fruit vote."

Just the South.

And I'm always a "Southern columnist," or "Southern humorist," or "that redneck from Atlanta."

Ever heard of Mike Royko being referred to as a "midwestern columnist"? Or Dave Barry, of *The Miami Herald*, a "Cuban columnist"?

If you're Southern, it's always going to be mentioned.

"Why don't you people forget the Civil War?" I've heard so often from Northerners.

Well, why don't y'all leave us the hell alone and stop thinking of the South as an odd appendage? How about stopping with the stereotyping already?

"The Bubba vote," indeed.

Allow me to explain "Bubba" once and for all:

"Bubba" normally comes from the fact little sisters have trouble saying "Brother." They have trouble with "Daddy" and "Mama," as well as "chrysanthemum," but that's another story. So "Daddy" comes out "Da-da" and "Mama" can come out "Mah-mah." But they don't normally stick.

But when "Brother" comes out something like "Bubba," it has a way of hanging on. "Bubba" is sort of cute coming out of a little sister's mouth, and pretty soon, the entire family is referring to the boy-child that way.

I'm not so sure it's an all-Southern, all-white thing. In fact, I'm certain it's not. Remember Bubba Smith, the football player who went to the pros and was last seen in one of those *Police Academy* movies? Bubba Smith attended Michigan State, and he's black. I have no idea how he got stuck with "Bubba," but they used to wear buttons at Michigan State football games that said, KILL, BUBBA, KILL.

Wasn't that racist? Didn't that portray a black man as nothing more than a violent machine that had no feelings and reacted to the smell of blood? If Bubba Smith had played at Ole Miss or at Georgia, you can bet some smarty-pants from *The*

New York Times would have taken "Kill, Bubba, Kill" and had a grand time with it, offering it as further proof of the backwardness and the racial insensitivity of the South.

I had a man write me a letter years ago with what he considered to be quite a dilemma. He had been called "Bubba" by his family and friends for thirty-five years. He came from a small Georgia town and had gone to work with a large national firm in Atlanta. His boss, he explained in the letter to me, had been transplanted from New York City.

"My boss called me into his office," the letter said, "and told me now that I held a high-level position with the firm, I could no longer use the name 'Bubba.'

"He said it sounded too 'Southern and ignorant.'

"But that's the way everybody knows me. I don't see a thing wrong with being called 'Bubba.' "

"Nor I," I wrote in a column regarding this situation.

And I was incensed the son of a bitch from New York City would say "too Southern and ignorant."

What if the man had been named "Booker T."? Would that have been too "black and ignorant"? How about "Lech" (as in Walesa), would that have been too "Polish and stupid"?

What if he had been named "Dances with Fat Girls"? "Too Indian and insensitive to persons of size"? How about "Bertrand"? Too "Jewish and cheap"?

What else I said, and felt, was that, quite frankly, I'd like to do business with a man named "Bubba." It's a name, I think, that says the person carrying it is honest, down-to-earth, and you could roll up your sleeves with him and dismiss with all pretensions and get whatever task was at hand done in a lot shorter time than if you were dealing with some guy named

"Vinny," which sounds "too New Yorky and the kind of guy who'd order a hit on you if you didn't like the sort of deal he was offering."

So I told the Bubba who wrote the letter to tell the jerk who wanted him to drop his name to kiss his ass and see if he could find a job with a firm that wasn't being run by a lot of Yankees who looked down on Southerners and had their heads in their asses (*cranial rectitus*).

I never heard from this particular "Bubba" again, but I did hear from a lot of other transplanted Yankees with *cranial rectitus* who delivered long diatribes concerning what was wrong with the South.

One wrote, "I was transferred to Atlanta from New York six years ago. Every time I return to Atlanta on an airplane, I expect the stewardesses to say, 'Welcome to Atlanta. Set your watch back two decades.'"

A woman wrote, "You Bubbas are all alike. All you can think about is football, beer swilling, and hillbilly music. I've been in Atlanta six years. I'm single and I'm college-educated, but I haven't met a single Southern male who reads without moving his lips."

My response to the first writer was "Oh, yeah? Every time I fly into New York, I expect the stewardess to say, 'Welcome to New York. Get off the plane at your own risk.'"

To the other, I responded, "Read this: Delta is ready when you are."

"Too Southern and ignorant . . ."

That makes my blood boil.

Allow me to get even here by doing a little stereotyping of my own. The Bubba vote? Okay, how about:

THE HONKER VOTE: Honkers are loudmouthed Yankees who never shut up, and they get that way because in the North, especially New York, everybody tries to talk at once (throwing their hands around), and the only way you can be heard is to be able to scream louder than everybody else taking part in the conversation.

Honkers sound like about eight zillion waterfowl, like ducks and geese, quacking and honking at once.

They pronounce "Bob" as "Baaa-b." And they always get cute with other people's names. Frankly, I don't like it when some honker tries to get familiar with me by calling me "Lew."

"It's 'Lewis,' " I want to say.

And "Nancy" can become "Nance," and "Vinny" can become "Vin," and "Mike" is "Mikey" and "Paul" becomes, inevitably, "Paulie."

Back off, you loudmouth Yankee son of a bitch. After we've known each other for a while and I've determined you have at least some sense, and you learn not to honk but to speak softly and not mock Southerners by using "you-all" in the singular sense, which is completely wrong because Southerners don't do that, I might allow you to become close enough to me, that if you mistakenly refer to me as "Lew," I might allow you to get away with it and say, "Please, it's 'Lewis,' " instead of "It's Lewis, goddammit."

But not before.

And, please, keep it down a few decibels, no matter what you are saying.

A friend of mine was describing what happened once when he was a spectator at the Masters golf tournament at the Augusta National Golf Club, where gentility has reigned for over fifty years.

This is a quiet place, a place of great beauty. There are azaleas and dogwoods. There is tradition and history. A sportscaster once referred to the Masters "gallery" as a "mob." He was never allowed by Masters officials (a committee of one, Cliff Roberts, who ran the tournament with an iron fist) to broadcast the tournament again.

Masters galleries for years have been referred to as "the most polite and knowledgeable" in golf.

My friend was sitting in front of the small pond that runs to the left of the par 3 sixteenth hole. It has been a favorite spot of galleries for years. Not only is it breathtakingly beautiful with the green of the turf, the green of the water, and the pinks and whites of the azaleas and dogwoods, it often has been the turning point of many Masters tournaments.

So my friend said, "I was sitting there with my wife, and these 'honkers' were sitting next to me. Not only were they loud, they used every golf cliché in the book and thought they were quite amusing.

"Nicklaus had an impossible putt from forty feet on a green that was like putting on the hood of a car. But he almost made it, leaving the ball just short on the lip. It was an incredible putt, but one of the honkers said, as aloud as he could, 'Never up, never in, Jackie!' and his buddies thought he was a riot. Everybody around him reacted to him as if he had just loudly broken wind.

"I had to get away from them for a while, and I decided to go to a concession tent for a beer. I'm standing there, and here come these idiots right behind me.

" 'Well,' one said when he reached the front of the line, 'what are we going to have to eat, fellows?'

"One of his buddies replied, after looking at the concession-stand list, 'Hey, that Masters sandwich sounds just delish—what about it, fellows?'

" 'Sounds terrif to me,' said the other honker, who then proceeded to ask the young black girl serving, 'Say, could you tell us what's in a Masters sandwich?'

"The girl said, 'There's some ham and some turkey and some roast beef, and some mayonnaise and some mustard, and some coleslaw and some pickles and some bread.'

" 'Sounds good to me,' said the first honker. 'Give us three Masters sandwiches.'

" 'We ain't got no mo'',' said the black girl.

"I nearly fell on the ground laughing."

Most honkers are from New Jersey, incidentally.

THE WHINY, BITCHY VOTE: Usually, these are Northern women, who talk through their noses a lot. The woman who couldn't find a Southern man who read without his lips moving was, in fact, a whiny-bitchette, I'm almost positive.

Whiny-bitchettes don't shave their legs or under their arms. They were all ugly in high school and could never get a date. When they do go out with guys, after they are older and learn to wash their hair occasionally, they usually go out with wimps and weenies from New York City named Bernie.

They also wear running shoes to work, wear glasses, and whine and bitch until they get off at five, and they all live with cats, which are whiny, bitchy animals.

They have names like Mona, and they have clammy-looking white skin and small breasts. "I wouldn't have intercourse with her with your male sexual organ" is what a Southern guy might say to his friend if he saw a whiny-bitchette.

THE WIMP AND WEENIE VOTE: These are Northern men who like Wally Cox. The "Mr. Peepers" vote. Bernies. Marvins. They marry whiny-bitchettes and produce more whiny-bitchettes, as well as wimps and weenies, who all wear thick glasses, go prematurely bald, and never take part in sports. They are too busy with their science projects and are too frail, anyway. They become editors of newspapers and college professors who are pissed at how much the head football coach is making, experts with computers whose eyes bug out of their heads eventually, liberal columnists, liberal lawyers, and politicians, and they take their ugly little whiny-bitchette wives to the beach once a year, and they wear Bermuda shorts and sandals and long black socks and can become terribly sunburned after three minutes' exposure to the sun. They're pissants, is what they are.

THE ROCKY VOTE: These are men who talk like Rocky Balboa and rarely make discernible, humanlike sounds. They say "duh" and "dis" and "dese" and "yo" a lot. They say, "Yo, Paulie, would yuh look at dis." Actually, they don't talk at all. They grunt. They wear black leather jackets, stupid-looking hats, and they all have greasy black hair.

They also usually have at least one tattoo, work in the shipping department, slobber a lot, do nothing more interesting on their off-time than stand around on street corners, making obscene remarks to female passersby. They are uneducated, uncouth, and they are greaseballs. A lot of them live in Philadelphia. More live in Newark, and New York City is full of them. If they aren't named Rocky, then they're Tony, Sal, or Dominick. A lot of them wind up in the Mafia.

THE HANG 10 VOTE: Idiots with blond hair who start every sentence with "I'm like," and for "she says," they say, "she goes," and they all live in southern California. You want stereotyping, I'll give you stereotyping. The male hang-tenners are all named Shawn or Kevin, and they've got sand for brains. The female hang-tenners all have names that end in *i*, like Debbi and Vicki and Poopi, and they are where all the blonde jokes come from. Hear about the blonde who had a pet zebra named Spot?

I could go on and on here. *Newsweek* can get away with using "the Bubba vote." But what if it offered a few of the ones I've mentioned before? It wouldn't, of course, because everybody who works for *Newsweek* is a creep or creepette who went to some school that has bad football teams and is either a wimp, a weenie, or a whiny-bitchette.

The poor Bubba/redneck/good ol' boy. Call us ignorant, racist, sexist, slovenly Neanderthals. We're the last group that hasn't risen up, formed some sort of coalition, and said, "You can't talk about us that way," because one of us would probably say, "One more word out of you, you little Yankee wimp faggot, and I'm gonna cut you," and that would be playing right into the hands of our detractors.

So what do we do? We take it, for the most part. Occasionally, one of us rises up, like me, but we are normally brushed aside as individuals still living in a sordid past of lynchings, queer-rollings, and Klan-rallyings, and who want to keep all women down—in addition to barefoot and pregnant—and make up the part of the nation H. L. Mencken once referred to as a "cultural Gobi," meaning we'd rather go to a rat-killing than a cultural performance.

A few words about that. H. L. Mencken was from Baltimore, and nobody from Baltimore has any right to cast aspersions on any other part of the country. Also, it was later discovered H. L. Mencken was guilty of at least some degree of anti-Semitism, the lousy hypocrite. And to think I actually wasted my time studying some of his writing in journalism school.

Also, I did go to my share of rat-killings in my youth. What you do is you go down to where the corn is stored at night and take positions with .22 rifles. Then somebody switches on a light, and the rats, which are eating the corn, are temporarily blinded, and you shoot as many of them as you can, thus helping save the corn.

But I also have seen Pavarotti live—once in New York and once in London. I have been to the Louvre, museums in such places as Vienna, and have eaten caviar at Maxim's in Paris. I enjoyed both ends of that spectrum, to be perfectly honest, and I'm probably located on the cultural pole somewhere in the midst of those two ends.

I enjoyed my rat-killing days, but I can sing along with Pavarotti when he sings "La donna è mobile." But I'm most at home now at a University of Georgia football game, a Willie Nelson concert, or a performance of *Miss Saigon* at the Drury Lane Theatre in London.

I do like caviar, but I like pork barbecue better. I attended an opera, *The Marriage of Figaro*, in Vienna and was quick to figure out that the whole thing was about how every guy in the cast had the hots for the rather plump lady's maid. I do admit leaving after the first act, but that was because it was too hot in the hall, and I thought I might faint.

I have two pairs of Gucci shoes in my closet, I wear Geoffrey Beene cologne, and I have a red Chevy Blazer that is six years old. I do not have a gun in a gun rack behind the front seat. I have a gun rack, but that's a four-iron, not a gun, that is resting in it.

And I will not, under any circumstances, turn my back on my heritage. I am proud of it, as a matter of fact, and I wouldn't have had it any other way.

Classified as a Redneck

Recently, I phoned the classified-ad department of the newspaper.

"Classified-ad department of the newspaper," a female voice said.

"I would like to take out a personal ad," I said.

"Can't get a date, huh?" the voice replied.

"Well," I answered, "it's just that I, uh . . ."

"You don't have to explain, dear. I've been doing personals for twenty years, and I've dealt with all kinds in my career," the voice went on. "Let's see, you're in your mid-forties, been divorced several times—three?"

"Three," I said.

"And there have been lots of girlfriends, but none of them have worked out. They spend all your money and are ungrateful to you, and what you want now is some twenty-three-year-old bimbette who has never heard of Montpelier, Vermont. Am I right?"

This was uncanny.

"Time is running out on me," I said, "and I'm afraid if I finally don't find a woman with whom I can have a long-standing relationship, I'm going to wind up alone in a nursing home."

"With a lot of hair growing out of your ears, and you'll drool a lot," said the woman. "I had a brother like that, the poor soul. He kept wanting to meet a woman who had been a home-ec major in college, because he liked to eat. He never found one, developed an ulcer in the process, and is now in a nursing home, and all he can eat is saltine crackers soaked in milk."

What a revolting picture. I had to find the right woman.

"So tell me what you want to say in your ad," the woman said. I told her.

"Oh, no," said my personals-ad counselor when I had finished.

"What's the matter?" I asked.

"Everything is the matter," she answered. "You're a SSWM, a straight Southern white male." The words came out of her mouth like she was spitting out rodent hairs.

"What's wrong with being one of those?" I asked her.

"Everything is wrong with being one of those," she said. "Straight Southern white males are the most politically incorrect individuals we have in nineties society. They are racists and sexists and gay-bashers. They are one step out of the Stone Age. They are fossils. They are obsolete. They just don't wash anymore. I wouldn't wish one on my worst enemy."

"Are you saying you aren't going to accept my ad?" I asked.

"Listen, you redneck," said the woman, her voice now dripping with venom, "if you've got the money, I'll run your ad, but you're wasting your time. No woman in her right mind would answer an ad to meet Slim Pickens. Why don't you just forget about this and save your money so you can go to a tractor pull with those other good ol' boys you hang around with?"

I was shocked beyond words. I was suddenly some sort of monster, some outcast? I always had been proud of my Southern heritage. My great-great-great-grandfather was the famous Confederate general Beauregard Grizzard, who had three horses and four Red Cross nurses shot out from under him during the Civil War and had lived through it all. After the war was over, he had opened a bait-and-beer store and sold more Pabst Blue Ribbon, red wigglers, and Louisiana pinks than any other bait-and-beer store in an eight-county area.

And, sure, I'm straight. I didn't even enjoy taking showers with other members of my basketball team when I was in high school. What could be wrong with that? Gay-basher? Me? At least I had learned to say "gay," rather than those other, more descriptive words we once used.

Then there was the racist thing. Just because you're a straight Southern white male, it doesn't necessarily mean you're racist, does it? My boyhood friend and idol, Weyman C. Wannamaker, Jr., was asked once if he was a member of the Klan.

"That's the rumor going around," he was told.

"You misunderstood," said Weyman. "Nobody said I was a member of the Klan. What they said was I'm a booger under the sheets."

I've never been a member of the Ku Klux Klan or any other racist group either, and I wouldn't even know where to go to buy one of those pointy-headed hats the Klansmen wear. The KKKmart? That would be my best guess.

And sexist. Just because I wanted a home-ec major so she can prepare me good things to eat? I would cook for myself, but I majored in journalism. The only thing they taught journalism students to cook up was a good angle to a story. I could still respect a woman who cooked dinner for me the next morning.

And allow me to say this: If a woman can do the same job as a man, she should be allowed to do it and receive equal pay. **DID YOU SEE THAT?** I'm not for keeping women barefoot and pregnant. I've been married three times, and not a single one of my wives ever got pregnant. I also happened to have bought my third wife a pair of five-hundred-dollar leather boots in the Gucci store in Florence, Italy, in 1980. A man who wanted to keep his wife barefoot certainly wouldn't shell out that kind of cash for a pair of boots. Most all women suffer from Imelda Marcos syndrome anyway—the desire to own, or at least try on, every pair of women's shoes on earth. Is that a sexist remark? If it is, I apologize, but I buy a pair of shoes and I wear them every day until they wear out. Then I go and buy another pair of shoes.

It has been my experience with women, however, that a closet without 416 pairs of shoes in it is like a necklace with no earrings to match.

But back to the barefoot thing for a moment. I must admit I don't see anything wrong with a woman taking off her shoes and feeling the terra firma on the bare underside of her feet, occasionally. It even can be a turn-on, an earthy sort of thing, like seeing a woman run naked through the forest. I've never seen a woman run naked through the forest, but it sounds like a lot more fun than going out there with a rifle, waiting for some poor unsuspecting deer to come along so I can shoot it and keep it from starving to death.

Kathy Sue Loudermilk, the sexiest girl in my school, didn't

even start wearing shoes until she was in high school, when the health teacher wrote a note to Kathy Sue's parents demanding they put shoes on her before she either got ringworm or stepped on a rusty nail and came down with lockjaw.

Kathy Sue didn't want to wear any shoes. She was one of the first let's-get-close-to-nature individuals I ever knew. She liked to feel the comforting red Georgia clay under her feet. She didn't even mind going to the henhouse to collect eggs for her mother and stepping in a neat pile of chicken leavings either.

I come from a rural, agricultural background myself, and I've known the feeling of stepping into chicken leavings, green with a touch of white right on top, while barefoot. While others might think such a thing was disgusting, the sensation actually is like stepping onto a pile of cool Jell-O pudding. It feels quite good to the area between the toes and makes a nice little squiggly sound, as in "Squiiiirglup," which is a combination of the words "Squirp" and "Squiggle." I actually once knew twin girls whose parents had named them Squirp and Squiggle, both of whom had a toe-sucking fetish, and there is nothing wrong with that. They later turned pro and opened a toe-sucking clinic, as a matter of fact, and were guests on a recent *Donahue* show where they discussed toe-sucking at length and even demonstrated their technique on Phil, who admitted he always had wanted his wife, Marlo, to suck his toes, but he had always been afraid to ask her.

"I want to thank Squirp and Squiggle," Phil closed his show, "for today's enlightening program. Tomorrow, our topic will be left-handed lesbian cross-dressers with rotten teeth."

Regardless of all that, however, I still had the problem of no woman in my life at the moment and the fact my personals counselor thought I and my kind were worse than a howling case of herpes.

Still, she had said if I had the money, she would run the ad, and I wasn't convinced I was some sort of social leper, despite what she had said.

So I told the woman, "Regardless of what you might think of straight Southern white males, my dear woman, I still want you to put the ad in the newspaper. I will pay for every inch of it, and we'll see just who can flush something out of the bushes and who can't."

"Such lovely phraseology," she replied, sarcastically. "The man thinks he's out with his dog, Ol' Gator, hunting prey."

I meant nothing by that. It was just the way I had learned to phrase certain things. I have already mentioned my lack of interest in going into the woods and shooting animals, but there shouldn't be anything wrong with an occasional allusion to the quest of game.

I'll never forget the time in the eighth grade when my boyhood friend and idol, Weyman C. Wannamaker, Jr., a great American, and I were watching Kathy Sue Loudermilk clean the chicken leavings from between her toes as she sat on the front steps of the schoolhouse before her first class one morning. The teachers insisted all barefoot children not track in any smells that would distract the other students.

Kathy Sue developed early as a child and, by the eighth grade, already had the wheels off her training bra. There she sat in a lovely dress her mother had made her from a Martha White flour sack. It seemed to cling to all the strategic positions. As Kathy Sue's lovely fingers caressed and cleaned between her darling little toes, her flour-sack dress had ridden up to her

thighs. Her hair had fallen down into her eyes, and she was holding her mouth in that pouty little way of hers. It was hard not to
believe in God looking at Kathy Sue that morning.

Weyman, spellbound for a moment, finally said, "I've been to
three county fairs, two square dances, and a Shriner parade. I've
seen a chicken play the piano, a baboon that knew his ABC's,
and a duck fart under water. But," he went on, nodding toward
Kathy Sue, "I ain't never seen a dog that'll hunt like that."

I finished the rather harrowing experience with the woman in
classifieds at the newspaper, who said my ad, as much as she
despised it, would run two days hence. The first day crawled by.
The anticipation was building in me with every minute that
passed. This could change my life. As soon as my ad appeared, I
was certain the letters would come pouring in, and I would have
the opportunity to choose from dozens of women who were
dying to meet me. And I wouldn't have to buy a single dinner or
drink. Why hadn't I thought of this earlier?

The morning of the day my personals ad was to appear, I was
up early waiting for the newspaper. I sat on my front porch pouring down coffee in the black of pre-dawn. Then, around the corner came a set of headlights. This is it. This was my newspaper
carrier. He slowed in front of my house, and from the driver's
side, he threw a perfect strike into the hedges in front of my
house.

I have some rather large hedges in front of my house, and
that's always where my carrier throws the newspaper. Sometimes, as was the case this particular morning, the paper would
fall down into the hedges, out of sight. My lawn was a lot bigger
target than my hedges, but newspaper carriers, I decided, are a
sadistic lot. If they had to get up at that time of the day to deliver newspapers, they seemed to want their customers to be

just as miserable, trying to disencumber their newspapers from remote and dangerous places such as inside large hedges or directly in front of the neighbor's sleeping pit bull named Attila.

It was still dark outside as the upper half of my torso disappeared into the hedges. I received multiple cuts to my face and hands, but after fifteen minutes of searching, I finally had my newspaper in hand.

I went inside, poured myself another cup of coffee. I glanced at the front page. The lead headline said:

ALIENS LAND IN NEW YORK CITY,
ARE MUGGED BY STREET GANGS

Another slow news day. I turned to the personals and began to search for mine. I found it. The ad directly above mine said:

"GWM: Seeking partner for fun and games. Must be physically fit, able to endure intense pain, and willing to experiment. Knowledge of power tools and animal husbandry helpful. Nonsmokers and Christians only."

The ad directly below mine said:

"BBIF: Fit, 30's bi-female truck driver seeks progressive guys and gals who enjoy travel and eating at truck stops. Big smokestacks and well-built rigs important. See what truckers really mean when they say they are going to 'blow the horn.' Carrying a heavy load, I'm waiting for you."

I got four responses the first day. The newspaper forwarded them from the P.O. box that ran in the ad.

One said, "Hey, trucker, I'm southbound and down. My CB handle is 'Big'un' and I love watered-down chili. Meet me at the bus station mornings 9–11 and afternoons 4–6. My leather lathers with anticipation."

Another read:

"I'm 6-2, 190, and if you're looking for a power tool, you've come to the right place. Black and Decker doesn't have anything on this nail driver. Pain's my game and I know chickens. Yours in Christ . . ."

Obviously, both these individuals had mistakenly written to the wrong P.O. box. A third letter wanted to sell me aluminum siding, and the fourth was a pyramid scheme to sell and breed llamas from South America.

It had to get better. It didn't. I ran that stupid ad for ten days, and I received only one more letter after the initial four. It was from Jimmy Swaggart, asking me for a donation.

Naturally, I was devastated. What had happened here? I hadn't advertised for anything weird. I didn't want to do anything that involved a farm animal or staple gun. I just wanted to meet that special lady who could take me out of the love nadir in which I presently found myself.

When I called the lady at the newspaper to tell her to cancel my ad, she obviously had something smart to say:

"What did I tell you, pig?" she began. "No woman in her right mind would answer an ad from an SSWM. They are afraid you'd ask them to do something sick, like go to a country-western bar. You rednecks are all alike. Your idea of foreplay is 'Get in the truck, bitch.' "

What could I say? She was right. If this had been a hunting expedition, all I would have gotten would've been chigger bites. If this had been a baseball game, I wouldn't have gotten a runner to first base. If it had been a war, I'd have been Iraq. If it had been a county fair, I'd have suffered whiplash on the Tilt-a-Whirl.

My ego had crashed. Even the black box with the cabin re-
corder had burned in the wreckage.

Here I was alone, and middle-aged, and a hair on a bar of
soap. An Arab at a B'nai B'rith meeting. A one-legged man at an
ass-kicking contest. Ford Pinto in a Rolls-Royce showroom. A
smoker at a joggers' picnic. A green fly in a bowl of soup. A piece
of porcelain at a Tupperware party. Ernest Tubb at a Guns N'
Roses concert.

I'd brought a knife to a gunfight. A date to a Ducks Unlim-
ited banquet. A mule to the Kentucky Derby. A voice of reason to a congressional debate. A cane pole to a deep-sea
fishing trip. Hitler to a meeting of the American Civil Liberties Union.

I was the epitome of politically incorrect. A redneck. A good
ol' boy. My name was Bubba. I drove a truck with a lot of
bumper stickers. One said AMERICA: LOVE IT OR LEAVE IT. Another read I BRAKE FOR BLONDES.

I wore a baseball cap with the name of a farm-implement
company on the front.

I went around saying things like "Anybody who don't like
Hank Williams can kiss my ass" and "Hey, little lady, can I buy
you a beer?" I enjoyed football more than long walks and baseball more than wine-and-cheese-tasting parties, and I lost interest in professional basketball when Bob Cousy retired.

I feared and despised welfare cheaters, rap, mushrooms,
anything that had to do with the Ivy League, fast-talking Yankees, married women who still went by their maiden names,
biscuits that come in a can, men wearing earrings and/or ponytails, San Francisco and New York City, liberal newspaper
columnists, Dan Rather, bikini underwear for men, and pho-

tography shows that feature a picture of a naked man with a bullwhip in his rectum.

With apologies to Jesse Helms, if that's art, my ass is a typewriter.

But what could I do about all this? I was too old, too set in my ways, and too stubborn in my beliefs to change. What are straight Southern white males supposed to do now that we've been cast aside like an old sofa? We're still a part of this society. I like to think we are still contributing to it. Who would change your oil and clean out your carburetor if it weren't for straight Southern white males?

Who would write country songs like a friend of mine is writing, with the title "I Can't Get Over You Until You Get Out from Under Him"?

Who would coach football at the University of Mississippi? Who would eat all the pork pig-barbecue sandwiches and drain all those longneck bottles of Bud? Who would be governor of Alabama? Who would love—with a nod to Tom T. Hall—old dogs, children, and watermelon wine? Who would put a car up on cement blocks in his backyard, go to stock-car races, and keep bait-and-beer stores in business, thus helping to stimulate the economy? Who would buy a pickled egg from the jar on the bar? Who would love truck stops and beer-joint waitresses and give them change to play Alan Jackson's "Don't Rock the Juke Box" on the jukebox?

Who would love and take care of sorry old dogs who sleep under trucks and get motor oil on their backs? Who would name bird dogs "Jim" and "Jesse" and own a decanter of bourbon in the shape of Elvis?

Who would say "I heard dat" and "Now, that's a nice 'un there, a real nice 'un" on televised fishing shows? Who would chew tobacco and carry around a paper spit cup with a napkin in it?

Who would still say "tote" for "carry," "sal-mun" for "sa-mon," and "bull-sheeyet" for "you don't say?"

Who? Tell me who?

Us. Straight Southern white males. We need love and understanding, too, and, once you get to know us, we aren't what the cat drug in from the garbage. We're people, too. We have feelings just like everybody else, and we're damn tired of being looked down upon and having our political ballots called "the Bubba vote."

I press onward.

Most of us work for our living. Some of us work very hard. We fly airplanes, sell used cars, heal the sick, build and design large buildings, change tires and pump gas, sing and play guitar, fight in wars, write books and plays, just to name a few of our occupations.

We also pay our bills and our taxes and provide for our families. In my case, I don't have a family, but I do take care of my dog, Catfish, the black Lab.

We normally are nice to our children, don't cheat on the golf course, give to charities, provide jobs for others, honor our parents, and give blood. Lest we forget, the father of our country, George Washington, was a straight white Southern male. And so is Dr. Billy Graham.

Certainly, we have a share of goofballs and ne'er-do-wells. What group, ethnic or otherwise, doesn't?

But we have one distinct, unifying factor. We don't know what's happened to the world, and there are a lot of things of which we are all sick and tired. I've mentioned whining and bitching. I'll mention it some more.

We're also tired of what we consider to be the chirping of little sparrows who don't have anything better to do than be disruptive and devious. I don't care if you're gay, just don't bother me with it. And what black millionaires get into what formerly all-white country clubs doesn't concern us in the least, and so you're suffering from PMS and are mad because Geraldine Ferraro never got elected vice president. We've got problems, too.

Like having to deal with the idiots in Congress who want to take and take from the productive in order to give and give to the unproductive, and having to be afraid of saying to a female employee "Good morning," and having her take it as sexual harassment and filing a lawsuit.

In a few words, we are confused and angry.

Damn right, I'm a straight Southern white male, and I got to be that way honestly, which is to say I'm proud of my heritage. It's politically incorrect by now to say such a thing, but I've already said what I thought about political correctness. I said it sucks the big one, if you don't recall, and if you think I'm enjoying speaking my mind here and telling the Speech Police to go to hell, you're right. This is more fun than playing with a pet chicken.

12 THE GOOD OL' DAYS

When Trash Was Garbage and People Were Normal

Mebbe the Front Porch Should Come Back

I was driving through the outskirts of the city the other day and I saw a man sitting on a front porch.

It was an older house and he was an older man. Modern houses don't have front porches anymore, and even if they did, younger men have far too much to do to sit on them.

I'm not certain when the front porch all but disappeared from American life, but it probably was about the same time television and air-conditioning were being installed in most every home.

Why sit out on the porch where it's hot and you can get mosquito-bit when you can sit inside where it's comfort-cooled and watch *Ozzie and Harriet*?

Even if an architect designs a porch today, it's usually placed in the back of the house where the hot tub is.

If we do venture out of our houses today, it's usually to get in the hot tub.

If Americans continue to spend all that time in their hot tubs, we may all eventually shrink down like the Lilliputians and become prunelike from boiling ourselves one too many times.

I grew up in my grandparents' home. They had a front porch; we spent a lot of time sitting on it.

My grandmother would shell butter beans. My grandfather would listen for trains.

"There comes the mail train to Montgomery," he'd say, pulling his watch out of his watch pocket. "She's running four minutes late."

I learned a lot sitting on the front porch with my grandparents. How to shell butter beans. How to find the Big Dipper. How to wait for a mosquito to alight and then slap that sucker dead. What a pleasure it is to listen for trains.

Our neighbors often dropped by and sat on the porch with us.

"It was awful what happened to Norvell Tenny, wasn't it?" a neighbor would say.

"What happened to him?" my grandmother would ask, looking up from her butter beans.

"Got three fingers cut clean off down at the sawmill."

Something else I learned on the front porch—not to include sawmilling in my future.

But even my grandparents eventually moved inside. They bought a television and enclosed the front porch and made it a den.

My grandfather enjoyed westerns. My grandmother never missed a Billy Graham sermon or a televised wrestling match. The mail train to Montgomery had to get along by itself after that.

Perhaps if front porches came back and people started sitting on them again, we'd learn to relax more and talk to one another more, and being bitten by a mosquito would at least be some contact with nature.

I probably should have stopped and talked to the old man on the porch and gotten his opinions on all of this.

I would have, too, but I was late for my tee time.

Difference Between Garbage and Trash

Did you know there was a difference between trash and garbage?

I'm nearly forty years old, and I didn't know that. I always figured trash and garbage were the same thing, a bunch of stuff you wanted to throw away.

You live, you learn.

The other morning I walked outside my house and noticed the can in which I dump my refuse (a highbrow word for a bunch of stuff you want to throw away) was still full from the previous day.

There was a little note stuck to the can. It said, in essence, that my refuse hadn't been picked up because—and I quote—"trash and garbage had been mixed."

I hate making mistakes like that. I didn't close the cover on a book of matches before striking. It was weeks before I got over the guilt.

I called Georgia Waste Systems, where I have my trash-garbage account, to apologize. They were very nice and said a lot of people make the same mistake I did and they were not planning a lawsuit.

As long as I had somebody on the phone who could explain, I asked, "What is the difference between trash and garbage?"

"Garbage," said a spokesindividual, "are things that come from the bathroom or kitchen."

"You mean like bread you leave out for a couple of months and green things start growing on it?" I asked.

"Precisely," she said.

"Trash," she continued, "is basically anything else. We do not pick up leaves, for instance, or old furniture, or boxes of materials that were collected when somebody cleaned out their attic."

The lady said it was up to the individual garbage collectors to decide if there is, in fact, trash and garbage mixed on their appointed rounds.

Somehow, I can't visualize two guys on a garbage truck really spending that much time trying to figure out which is which.

"What is it you have there, Leonard? Is it trash or garbage?" one guy says to the other.

"I can't be absolutely certain, Elvin, but it has green things growing on it."

I will, of course, comply with the waste company's dictum against mixing my trash and my garbage, but don't we have enough complexities in our lives as it is?

Don't we have to deal with international terrorism and the women's movement? Don't we have to battle traffic, computer involvement in our lives and airplanes that never take off on time?

Isn't it enough of a burden that we have to decide what to do about Central America, which long-distance telephone company we want to serve us and which cereal has the most fiber?

Oh, for a simpler time, when the good guys won, a girl could still cook and still would, and trash and garbage were the same, both delicacies as far as a goat was concerned.

It is a wonder that more of us don't tie a Glad bag around our heads and tell modern living to go stick its head in the nearest Dumpster.

Modernizing Monopoly

I ran into my friend Rigsby coming out of a department store. He had been buying Christmas gifts for his nieces and nephews.

"What did you get the little angels?" I asked.

"Games," he replied. "I picked up the updated versions of Clue and Monopoly."

"Updated?"

"Of course. This is the eighties, and kids today simply couldn't relate to the way we used to play Clue and Monopoly."

"How have they been updated?" was my next question.

"Well," said Rigsby, "in Clue the rooms in the house have been changed. The lounge is now the rec room, the bedroom is the owner's retreat, the library becomes the video room and what was once the ballroom is now the spa, with sauna and whirlpool.

"The weapons are new, too. They don't have the rope, the wrench, the lead pipe anymore. Too primitive. There's now a choke wire, an assortment of flying Ninja weapons and a switchblade. The revolver is a Saturday night special, and they've thrown in a mail-order Uzi submachine gun."

"How about the characters?"

"Basically, they're the same, but more intriguing. As a matter of fact, one might now use fiber evidence to prove that Blane, the illegitimate result of an illicit affair between Colonel Mustard and Miss Scarlett, murdered his victim by throwing an electric vibrator into the hot tub."

"Exciting," I said. "How has Monopoly changed?"

"For starters," said Rigsby, "the tokens are no longer the same. Instead of an old car, a top hat and a ship, there's now a nuclear submarine, a running shoe, a miniature DeLorean and a cruise missile.

"They've done away with the giveaway programs, too. There's a topless nightclub where Community Chest used to be.

"Baltic and Mediterranean were razed and casinos were built. If you land there on a roll of seven or eleven, you win money. If not, the house takes the two hundred dollars you just got for passing Go."

"What about railroads and utilities?"

"The government bailed out Reading Railroad, but the other three had to go the Chapter Eleven route. And watch out if you land on the Electric Company. They've just gotten a 26 percent increase on rates because of the cost overruns on the nuclear power plant they built where Free Parking used to be.

"Plant San Andreas is located there now, and if you land on it, it costs you twenty dollars to rent a radiation suit. Also, you have to pay twenty dollars for bottled water if you land on Ventnor Avenue because there was a toxic waste dump built there, and some of the waste seeped into the reservoir at Water Works next door."

"Sounds like the updated version of Monopoly is really an adventure now," I said.

"I'll say," Rigsby agreed. "I played a game with friends recently and I was doing pretty good until the other players found a minute amount of cocaine in the trunk of my DeLorean token."

"Did you have to go directly to jail?"

"No," said Rigsby. "I got out of it because they forgot to read me my Miranda rights."

Breakfast in New Orleans

NEW ORLEANS—I went down for breakfast from my room in the Fairmont Hotel. New Orleans, I might add, is still here after hosting the Super Bowl and the annual showcase for mental illness known as Mardi Gras.

I ordered what I always order for breakfast—grits, toast, bacon, two eggs medium-well and a Tab. (I realize most people start their days with coffee or orange juice, but I drink Tab, which certainly isn't as weird as some of the other stuff I do.)

As usual, I went over how to cook eggs medium-well with my waitress.

"I want the white completely done—I don't want any of it to ooze—and I want the yellow almost done, but not quite. Rather than running, I want the yellow to crawl."

I sipped on my Tab and glanced through the morning paper, awaiting my breakfast.

The big story in New Orleans was whether or not the state will legalize casino gambling. I'm all for it. Sin was invented in New Orleans. What's one more?

The waitress brought my eggs. I knew by looking at them they were prepared incorrectly. The yellow had been left on the heat far too long and it wasn't running or crawling. It was just sort of sitting there, hard as Chinese arithmetic.

"These eggs aren't what I ordered at all," I said. "The yellow is overcooked."

The waitress was very pleasant.

"I will take them back," she said.

In a very few moments she returned with my eggs and this time they were prepared perfectly.

"I'm so sorry," she said, "but I punched in your order incorrectly on the computer."

For a moment, I thought she said she had punched in my order incorrectly on a computer.

That's exactly what she said.

"You have a computer that you tell how a customer wants his eggs cooked?" I asked, shocked at the very notion of such a thing.

"We recently modernized our kitchen," the waitress replied.

How long, America, oh, how long are we going to stand for computers creeping more and more into things we hold dear, such as breakfast?

What happened to ordering breakfast, and the waitress hollering at the cook—a guy named Earl with tattoos on his arm— "Gimme a Number Three, crawling, a side of burned pig, Aunt Jemima's, roll it in dough with one of them sissy Co-Colers!"

The breakfast was delicious, but that is not the point here. The point is I do not want a computer involved in any fashion whatsoever with things I eat.

Computers have caused me enough trouble, losing my hotel reservations, my airplane tickets and payments to the electric company.

"How was your service?" the cashier asked me when I went to pay my bill.

"The computer botched my egg order," I said.

"We've been having some trouble with it," she replied. "Yesterday, it was gone for an hour and a half and came back wearing a tattoo."

Hearing that made me feel a lot better.

Recalling My School Daze

A young woman was expelled from a Goldsboro, North Carolina, high school recently because she modeled a bathing suit in a shopping mall.

A judge later ruled the student, seventeen-year-old Michelle Outlaw, could return to school, however, and justice certainly was served.

High school kids are walking around with green hair, so what's the big deal about modeling a bathing suit?

Kathy Sue Loudermilk, hallowed be her name, entered a Miss Collard Festival beauty pageant back home one year and wore a bathing suit that was much too small to hold everything Kathy Sue had attempted to stuff into it.

During the talent portion of the contest, Kathy Sue was doing her famous "Dueling Kazoos" number, and her suit gave way and split right down the front.

Parents attempted to cover their children's eyes, and the Baptist minister had to be revived with cold water.

Said my boyhood friend and idol, Weyman C. Wannamaker, Jr., a great American, who witnessed the incident, "What kazoos!"

I can't imagine a student being expelled from school for simply modeling a swimsuit. Students were expelled back when I was in high school for sure, but you had to do some heavy-duty rotten stuff to get the gate.

Weyman was expelled for one of the classics of teenage vandalism. He put cherry bombs down each of the three commodes in the boys' room and then flushed.

By some method I'm not certain of, cherry bombs will explode underwater. Not only was the boys' room completely flooded, but they found pieces of broken commode all the way down at the tether-ball pole on the playground.

Weyman's father, Mr. Wannamaker, of Wannamaker Plumbing, gave the school a 10 percent discount on what he charged for cleaning up the mess. It was considered a fine gesture.

Frankie Garfield, the school bully, usually was expelled once a week. Among other things, he once set fire to the school library in an effort to get out of having to read *Les Misérables*. The book was damaged, however. And rumor had it Frankie actually read four pages before his dog, Killer, ate the book.

Frankie also stole a pig and brought it to school in a sack. He set the pig free in the home-ec lab where the students were learning to fry bacon. Three of the girls, thinking the pig was bent on revenge, fainted.

Frankie got expelled, but the pig fared even worse. It ate a sponge cake the home-ec class had prepared, got sick, and died.

Back to Kathy Sue: She fared a lot better than Michelle Outlaw, too. Not only was she not expelled, a ceremony was held and what was left of Kathy Sue's swimsuit was placed on display at the local feed store, which sponsored the Miss Collard Festival pageant.

I guess we were just a lot more liberal back then.

The Filth They Call Music

A man who said he had two teenage daughters wrote and asked if I would comment on, as he put it, "the filth they're selling as music these days."

So happy to oblige, and I must agree with the man that the filth they are selling as music these days isn't really music, just a guy with a deep voice saying a lot of dirty words while somebody beats on a barrel with a two-iron and somebody else kills a cat in the background.

Music music at least should have a tune so you can hum it while you kill a cat.

Also, the man who wrote isn't the only person who is concerned about the filth they are selling as music these days.

The governor of Florida is concerned, for instance. He wants the state's prosecutor to find a way to keep a recording by something called The 2 Live Crew away from minors.

I saw a photograph of The 2 Live Crew in the paper. They were four young men who looked more like somebody's starting backfield than a recording group, but what do I know?

Bette Midler looks more like a linebacker than a singer, but she did a pretty good job on "Wind Beneath My Wings."

The 2 Live Crew has a blockbuster hit out titled "Me So Horny." I have never heard the recording, but *The Washington Post* called it "a misogynist's catalog of aggressive sexual acts, delivered in lewd and lurid detail."

Translated, that means the lyrics are so filthy you would be appalled if you heard them, thus making your teenage daughters drool for the first opportunity to get their hot little ears on them, too.

What I think is people like the governor of Florida and the man who wrote me are wasting their time.

That's because there is an ageless equation that goes "Nothing sells like controversy."

There's this guy in New York named Bernie, see. He works for a record label. He wears a toupee and a jewelry store around his neck.

When The 2 Live Crew first brought their recording to him, it was titled "The Wind in Your Hair."

But Bernie's smart. He said to The 2 Live Crew, "That won't sell eight copies. Call it 'Me So Horny' and make it filthy and get back to me in thirty minutes."

So, The 2 Live Crew puts out a misogynist's catalog of aggressive sexual acts, delivered in lewd and lurid detail, parents get upset, the governor of Florida gets upset, and kids flock to record stores to buy it, and Bernie gets rich and the recording group gets rich.

Legislation won't stop the aforementioned equation from working. All that will stop it is to ignore The 2 Live Crew and "Me So Horny," thus taking away the thrill your kids get when they listen to such.

That way, your children will go back to dyeing their hair orange, or whatever else they can think of to drive you crazy, and The 2 Live Crew will sign with Clemson, and Bernie will have to find a real job.

Like being a pimp.

Yo . . . Can You Cap This?

Add this to the long list of things I don't understand about modern culture:

Why are so many of today's young men wearing their ball caps backward?

Surely others have noticed this, too. I don't have any scientific figures, but I would be willing to guess that at least 75 percent of young men who wear ball caps are wearing them backward.

I used to wear ball caps. But I always wore them the way I figured God and whoever invented ball caps intended—with the bill in front so as to keep the sun out of my eyes and off my face.

The only person who wore his ball cap backward was the catcher. He had to turn his cap around in order to wear his face mask.

But when he wasn't behind the plate, he turned his cap around like everybody else.

Wearing ball caps backward seems to have no racial lines. I've seen both young black and white men wearing their ball caps backward.

I stopped a young black man and asked why he was wearing his ball cap in such a manner.

He said, "Yo."

So I stopped a young white man and asked him the same question.

He said, "Yo," too.

I'm not certain what "yo" means.

Perhaps it means, "I am making a statement that says I refuse to adhere to ancient customs of adults, and if I want to wear my ball cap backward, I will continue to do so, yo."

Later I saw a young man wearing his ball cap with the bill in front.

I said, "Does this mean you are not making a statement and refusing to adhere to ancient customs of adults?"

He said, "Yo, I knew something didn't feel right," and turned his ball cap around backward.

I still have an old ball cap. I keep it around for sentimental reasons. I was wearing that cap when my high school baseball coach came to the mound one day when I was pitching and said,

"Grizzard, you couldn't get your grandmother out. Get off the mound."

I put my old ball cap on my head and then turned it around with the bill in the back. I looked like a skinny Yogi Berra, or Joe Garagiola when he still had his hair.

I turned it back around. I looked like a forty-three-year-old man who couldn't have gotten his grandmother out.

I've come to a couple of conclusions in this matter.

One is that I probably shouldn't question the customs of the younger generation in the first place. My generation, when it was still young, made its own statements. We wore ducktails and rolled up our Lucky Strikes in our shirt sleeves. We were trying to say, "My, but is that Jerry Lee Lewis a piano-playing fool?"

And two, young men who wear their ball caps backward probably should carry a card around in their wallets that says, "If I have been injured and rendered unconscious, please don't try to turn my head around."

Yo, you never know.

Up the Creek with Bottled Water

They found out some bottles of Perrier had benzene in them, and now Perrier drinkers are afraid to drink the stuff. Ha. Ha. Ha.

I'm laughing because I think Perrier is stupid and anybody who drinks Perrier is stupid.

You know what Perrier is? It's water that bubbles out of a spring in France somewhere. I've seen people—usually in their twenties and thirties who spend their weekends biking around in their tight biking britches—go into those fancy bars and order Perrier for $3.50 a pop.

They apparently think Perrier, since it's from France and comes in a bottle, is better for them than regular American water that comes out of a regular American tap.

And some of these people order Perrier on the rocks, which is water over ice, and the ice is made from, you guessed it, tap water. These people ride tricycles.

My late father was one of the great ice-water drinkers of all time. He drank a lot of other stuff, too, which is perhaps why he was always thirsty for ice water.

Anyway, whenever he stopped for gasoline, he would ask the station attendant, "Do you have any ice water?"

One day, we stopped and my father asked for ice water, and the attendant brought it out and said, "That'll be a dime."

"You're charging me for ice water?" my father asked, shocked beyond belief.

He gave the water back to the man, called him a communist son-of-a-pig, and off we drove.

Can you imagine what my father would have thought about people paying $3.50 for a glass of water in one of those bars where the guys all wear suspenders?

Water used to be simple. There was well water. You just dug a hole on your property until you hit water.

Your Ol' Uncle Lewis here can remember getting a drink of water by lowering a bucket into the well with a rope.

Well water was always cold, never made anybody sick that I know of, and it was free.

Ol' Uncle Lewis also can remember when you could drink water out of a creek. There was a creek on Red Murphy's property, and what a creek it was.

Because there were no Nintendo games or crack, we used to dam the creek about twice a week for fun and to get high.

The creek was fed by a spring. If you got thirsty while damming the creek, you went over to the spring, got down on your belly, stuck your mouth to the water, and drank your fill.

There are still springs, but I wouldn't drink out of any of them anymore. If there's not benzene floating around, there's probably worse.

My premise here is that although there might be some chemicals in your tap water, it must still be safe to drink, given all the modern purifying techniques of city waterworks.

And to pay some ridiculous price for a bottle of water shipped all the way from France by people you don't even know is, well, like I said earlier, stupid—benzene or no benzene.

By the way, if you are now, or have ever been before, a Perrier drinker, you may have some benzene in you.

Know what benzene causes? It causes your butt to get huge so it won't fit into your tight bike britches anymore.

Ha. Ha. Ha.

13 HEALTH

Hints, the Hospital, and a Lot of Heart

Going Up in Smoke

My friend Rigsby, the entrepreneur, currently is hatching another of his get-rich-quick schemes.

He sounded excited when he told me about his idea over lunch.

"You heard smoking is now banned on all commercial flights in California, didn't you?" he asked.

I said I had. There was a near riot aboard a TWA jet when smokers rebelled against the new antismoking law.

"And things are just going to get worse," Rigsby went on. "After April, smokers will not be allowed to light up on any flight anywhere in the country of two hours or less. There are going to be a lot of uncomfortable smokers flying around up there."

I agreed, but I wanted to know where all this fits in with Rigsby's new idea.

"An all-smokers' airline." He beamed.

"I don't understand," I said.

"It's simple," Rigsby explained. "I'm going to lease some airplanes and start a new airline for smokers only.

"You can smoke all you want on my airline. In fact, I will encourage smoking. Flight attendants will carry cigarettes up and down the aisle like the girls in Vegas. I'll charge five bucks a pack. A smoker who runs out of cigarettes on an airplane is a desperate individual who will pay anything for another pack."

I admitted the idea had some promise.

"What are you going to call your airline?" I asked Rigsby.

"I've got my marketing staff on that now," he said. "We're thinking of something that will really catch the smoking public's attention. 'Black Lung Airlines' was one thought."

"I don't think so," I said.

"Then how about 'Air Emphysema'?"

"Keep trying."

"Okay," said Rigsby, "but let me tell you what else I'm going to offer on my all-smokers' airline.

"First we're going to make certain no nonsmokers come aboard and make life miserable for our customers. We will check each passenger's teeth and fingers. If they aren't yellow from smoking, they don't get a boarding pass.

"We're not going to fly high enough to need cabin pressurization, so our passengers won't have to worry about ever having to use those oxygen masks and not being able to smoke.

"Our flight crew will all be smokers, as well as our flight attendants, mechanics, reservationists, and boarding agents."

"But," I asked, "won't all that smoking make it uncomfortable on the plane?"

"Of course not," said Rigsby. "Smokers love smoke, and we're going to issue a miner's hat with the little light on the front so passengers can find the lavatories regardless of how thick the smoke is in the cabin."

"When will your ad campaign begin?" I asked my friend.

"Shortly," he said.

"What's your hook?"

"It's a great one—'An all-smokers' airline, here to serve you just in the nick of teen.' "

Who am I to scoff? They laughed at Wilbur and Orville, too.

Six Steps to Stop Smoking, Butt Don't Stumble

Since I wrote of my successful effort in quitting smoking, I have had many letters and calls.

They fit into two categories:

- One group said, "You lying sleazebag. You didn't quit smoking."
- The other group wanted to know, "How on earth did a weak individual such as yourself find the self-control to quit smoking?"

I will address the first group by saying, "Yes, I did quit smoking. I still want a cigarette, I dream about cigarettes, and if anybody comes out with a cigarette that won't kill me, I'll start smoking them again."

I want to answer the second group by replying, "Even the weakest individuals, such as me, can quit smoking, too, if they follow my step-by-step stop-smoking plan, which is absolutely free and doesn't involve chewing any gum or taking any shots or medicine or getting hypnotized."

Here is how to quit smoking, my way:

STEP 1: Get aboard some type of public conveyance that doesn't allow smoking and light up a cigarette. When nonsmokers begin to harass you, ignore them and keep on smoking.

Nonsmokers are violent, revenge-bent people. At some point, one of these people will come over to you, take your cigarette out of your mouth, crush it on the floor, and hit you somewhere in the region of your head.

Also realize it won't be that much longer until nonsmokers will begin shooting smokers in the streets. Now, you're on the way to being smoke-free.

STEP 2: Soon the stitches are out and your bruises are healed, but you're getting the urge to smoke again.

Buy a pack of cigarettes, take one out of the pack, and light it. Now, instead of putting the unlit end in your mouth, do it the other way. It will take those blisters on your tongue weeks to heal, and during that period, you won't want a cigarette.

STEP 3: The next time you get the urge to smoke, go buy a pack of Larks. I'm not even certain they make Larks anymore, so if you can't find a pack, try smoking a piece of shag carpet instead—it's about the same thing.

STEP 4: Invite Surgeon General Koop over for dinner. After eating, light up a cigarette and explain how much casual sex you've been having lately, and how you think condoms are a silly waste of time. The Surgeon General will begin screaming at you and breaking up your furniture. This man is serious about cigarettes and condoms.

STEP 5: Recall that John Wayne smoked; and cigarettes got him when 8 zillion Japanese couldn't.

STEP 6: The final step. Before going to bed one evening, open a beer and drink half of it.

Then light a cigarette and smoke it and throw the butt into the half-empty beer can. In fact, smoke a couple more cigarettes and put them out in the beer can.

Let it sit overnight.

The next morning before you do anything else, find the can and take a big swallow of the warm beer with the soggy cigarettes in it.

If you still want to smoke after that, then there's nothing I, or anybody else, can do for you, Pilgrim.

The Comedy of Eros

A friend was telling me a story about his elderly parents.

"Daddy's eighty-one," he began. "And Momma's seventy-six.

"Daddy went to the doctor and found out he might have prostate cancer. He was supposed to have a lot of tests done, and I asked my own doctor what sort of prognosis I could expect if Daddy's tests were positive.

"He said, 'I really don't know why they would do a lot of tests on your father. They're not about to operate on him at his age. Prostate cancer moves so slowly, he'll likely die of something else before the cancer has time to do it.'

"Anyway, the doctors went ahead and did the tests, and they did find prostate cancer in Daddy, but, like my doctor said, there would be no operation.

"But Momma called me again and seemed a little worried. She said, 'Son, there's something your daddy and me want you to find out for us.'

"I said, 'What is it?'

"She said, 'Well, our doctor at home is just so young we didn't want to ask him. But do you mind asking your doctor if, with Daddy's condition, is it still safe for us to have sex?' "

I have another friend whose father, a widower, was in his mid eighties when he was diagnosed as having cancer of the testicles. An operation was scheduled to removed them.

"Daddy worried and worried about it," said my other friend.

"I said, 'Daddy, you'll do just fine.'

"He said, 'I'm not worried about the operation, I'm worried about what's going to happen to my social life if I live through it.' "

I know another man who's well into his eighties. He's a widower, too. He's slim, tan, and he still has a full head of white hair.

He's a regular in the singles' bars, despite his age. He still even makes a move now and then. Once I asked him, "How can you stay this interested at your age?"

"For one thing," he answered, "I've never eaten any vegetables."

My grandmother described the night my grandfather died. He was seventy-three.

"We had just gone to bed and all of a sudden, he turned over on top of me and started kissing me. He hadn't kissed me that way in years. Then, I felt his arms, which were around me, loosen. He died that way, in our embrace."

Earl and Phil were up into their eighties. As lifelong friends they made a pact that whoever died first would come back and tell the other what heaven was like.

Earl died and then came back to Phil as he slept one night.

"Phil," he said, "this is Earl."

"Earl! You're back! Tell me what it's like!"

"Well," said Earl, "I get up in the morning and eat and then I have sex until noon.

"Then I eat lunch and take a nap and have sex for the rest of the afternoon. After that, I eat supper and have some more sex and then I go to sleep."

"So that's what heaven's like," said Phil.

"I'm not in heaven," said Earl. "I'm a jack rabbit in West Texas."

The older I get, the more I appreciate such stories.

Ex–Health Nut Breaks for Breakfast

My friend Rigsby, the health nut, had that look in his eye.

"I did it," he said.

"Did what?" I asked him.

"I had breakfast."

"So did I," I said. "What's the big deal?"

"I had a real breakfast," Rigsby answered. "For ten years all I've had for breakfast are things that are supposed to be good for me.

"I've eaten enough oat bran to qualify for the Kentucky Derby. I've eaten more yogurt than a hundred-and-twelve-year-old Russian. I've eaten so many bananas on my granola, I'm growing hair on my back and twice a day have a serious urge to go hang upside down on a tree limb."

"But breakfast is our most important meal," I said. "You should be eating healthy in the morning."

"I don't care," said Rigsby. "Man can't live on fiber alone. He must also have an occasional scrambled egg."

"You ate an egg?" I asked him in disbelief.

"Four," Rigsby answered.

I don't remember the last time I had an egg. I think it was during the Eisenhower administration.

"Aren't you afraid of getting too much cholesterol?" I asked Rigsby.

"I've got to die of something, and if an egg doesn't get me, something else will."

"What else did you have?"

"A Belgian waffle," said Rigsby. "With butter and syrup all over it."

"That's a lot of sugar. What about hypoglycemia?"

"What about it?"

"Well," I attempted to explain, "you could become faint, disoriented, and develop diabetes."

"Yeah," said Rigsby. "I could also get run over by a beer truck, but I'm still going to cross the street."

"Did you eat anything else?"

"I had some bacon."

"Bacon, studies show, can cause cancer."

"And I ate some white toast."

"No nutritional value there. You should have eaten whole wheat."

"And some pancakes."

"On top of the Belgian waffle? Are your affairs in order?"

"And some hash brown potatoes."

"All that grease. Who's the executor of your will?"

"And three chocolate doughnuts."

"You won't live until Christmas."

"And some leftover pizza from the night before."

"Our Father, who art . . ."

"And a Little Debbie Snack Cake."

"We're going to miss you."

"And a pot of coffee."

"Decaf, of course."

"High test."

"I'm looking at a dead man."

"And you know what else?" Rigsby asked me.

"What else?"

"I'm going to do it again in the morning."

It takes a real man, I suppose, to stare death square in the eye. I think I'll go over to the Waffle House and drool.

Body Language

My body and I had a long talk the other morning. First, my heart asked, "What's that you're drinking?"

"Coffee," I said, adding, with some degree of pride, "but it's decaffeinated. Caffeine is bad for me, so I've cut it out."

"Uh-oh," said my heart.

"What do you mean?" I asked.

"You haven't heard," replied my heart. "A new study has indicated decaffeinated coffee is made from beans that can cause bad cholesterol. You keep drinking that stuff, and my arteries will clog up and we'll buy the farm."

I already had cut down on eggs to help reduce my cholesterol count. Now, I'm told decaffeinated coffee, which I thought was good for me, picks up where the eggs leave off.

"One other thing," said my heart, "you know how you often get up in the middle of the night and go downstairs and eat some raw zucchini?"

"Raw vegetables are good for me," I said.

"That may very well be," said my heart, "but another new study says getting up suddenly in the middle of the night can cause a heart attack."

"So no more midnight raw zucchini?"

"No more," said my heart.

My colon piped up.

"What's that you're eating?" it asked.

"Cereal," I said. "I'm doing it for you."

"What's that cereal made from?"

"Healthy grains of corn, I suppose," I answered.

"Uh-oh," said my colon.

"What's the problem?"

"You should be eating cereal made from oat bran. It's better for me than what you're eating now."

"Who says?" I asked my colon.

"The people who sell oat bran."

I was getting discouraged.

My blood joined in.

"You're not actually going to eat that cinnamon roll, are you?"

"I love cinnamon rolls," I answered. "What's wrong with a cinnamon roll?"

"Sugar," said my blood. "Eat too much sugar and we'll have to deal with hypoglycemia."

"Dang right," said my pancreas.

"But I drink diet soft drinks, to cut down on my sugar intake," I said.

"Yeah," my blood said. "You and all those dead laboratory rats."

Just then my stomach joined in the conversation.

"Since eating fish can prevent cancer, when am I going to get some more fish?" asked my stomach.

"I'm afraid to eat any more fish," I said. "I saw a report on television saying to be careful about eating fish because the government wasn't doing a very good job inspecting it and I could get hepatitis."

"Big deal. You want me to get cancer?" my stomach asked.

After that, I made a few decisions.

I decided I wouldn't drink any sort of coffee anymore, I'd eat cereals made only of oat bran, I'd cut out all sugars—both real and artificial—I'd call in twelve government inspectors to look over any fish I was about to eat, and I would never, under any circumstances, get up at midnight, which could cause me to have a heart attack.

(If my house catches on fire at midnight, I'll cross that bridge when I come to it.)

Then I thought, What if I do all that and radon gas seeps into my house and kills me?

I went to the refrigerator, pulled out a nonalcoholic beer, and had myself a good cry.

A Flash and the Pan

Everybody knows about hospital gowns. They have no back to them. I explained earlier that this is to make it very uncomfortable for the patient while lying on a cold steel table. It is also so they can give you a shot in your butt quickly and get a bedpan in the correct position before any sort of accident can take place that gives a hospital laundry room fits.

The problem with a man wearing a gown, however, is that most men don't wear gowns at any other time except when they are in hospitals. Men who wear gowns at other times march in a lot of parades these days, but this is no time to go into that.

What a gown does when being worn in a hospital bed is ride up. With no tugging involved whatsoever, it just sort of rides up when you aren't looking. You don't wear any underwear under your gown in a hospital, so, to be perfectly blunt about it, the whole world gets a number of shots at your testicles.

I didn't mean for anybody to have a look at my testicles, but it just happened. I would kick my covers off, my gown would ride up, and Dedra would say, "For God's sake, Lewis, pull your gown down. Everybody can see your testicles."

To be perfectly honest about it, I really didn't care if anybody saw my testicles. The nurses, for instance. Imagine how many testicles they had already seen over their careers. It's something they ask all nursing candidates as they enter nursing school.

"You aren't getting into this line of work just so you can see testicles, are you?"

All nurses answer, "Of course not." I imagine some are lying, but they usually wind up working in sperm banks. I actually talked to a nurse once who worked for a urologist; she said she would peek through the door to watch men masturbate into condoms when they had to have their sperm checked. (I'm sorry. I was supposed to be delicate, wasn't I?)

It doesn't take you long in a hospital to lose most of your dignity, anyway. You check it at the admitting office.

"We'll take your dignity now," says the admitting nurse. "Just leave it right here on the desk. We'll give it back when you are discharged."

But I was embarrassed later when Dedra said that a minister came to see me with his wife, and she was one of those who got a free shot. Apparently, I also bared my testicles during a visit by a woman delivering flowers and balloons to my room. Not to mention that I'd flashed the entire hospital public-relations staff, who had visited me to beseech me not to give the *National Enquirer* the story about my peeing on Dr. Martin's shoes.

"The entire staff?" I asked.

"All of them," said Dedra.

I would like to take this opportunity to apologize and ask the obvious question: When will medical science invent a suitable codpiece to avoid such situations?

Now that I have discussed showing my testicles, I figure just about anything goes, but I am still trying to remain soft core here:

Intensive care is bedpan alley. After you are released from

there, you have to do it all in the rest room. You have to get out of your bed and walk (in my case, with a walker. I wasn't hoofing it that well as yet) into the rest room.

Number one is no problem whatsoever. Number two is. With all the cutting that was done on my chest, I didn't have a great deal of reach. Do I have to paint a clearer picture here? I think not.

Suddenly, you're four years old again and haven't learned your way around a roll of toilet paper. Mom did that for you, remember? You said, "Mom, I'm through," and in she came to finish things off.

You have to do that in the hospital after heart surgery, too. Imagine a forty-six-year-old man having to shout out, "I'm through," and in comes a nurse.

I didn't attempt to carry on a conversation with any of the nurses while any of this was taking place. I didn't think it was any time for chitchat, and I am certain they all appreciated that.

But I wondered to myself, Do they tell nurses—after they ask about the testicles—they might have to do this sort of thing following graduation?

If they do, I wonder just how many people get run out of nursing and go into demolition, upholstery repair, or selling aluminum siding as a result?

I hereby bow in behalf of and thank all nurses who had to do that to me while I was recuperating in Emory Hospital. As long as I am alive, yours is not a thankless task.

Grave Affairs

I had not put any thought into my funeral plans before my third heart operation; I suppose I just subconsciously ignored it all. But Dedra said I awakened one Monday morning in the hospital with it very much on my mind.

"You asked me to come into the bathroom with you and bring a pen and paper," she said. "Once we got inside, you said, 'Write all this down. This is what I want, in case I die.'"

She kept the paper. She showed it to me after I'd returned home from the hospital.

I had decided I wanted to be cremated after all. I had wanted my ashes spread over Sanford Stadium, on the campus of the University of Georgia. I had told Dedra that if she couldn't get permission, to sneak in at night and do it. I'm certain the Georgia Athletic Department gets a lot of requests like that, and if they allowed everybody who wanted his or her ashes strewn over the field, it eventually would do harm to the lovely turf.

I said I wanted to have a memorial service of sorts, held outdoors on the first tee at the Ansley Golf Club in Atlanta, where I am a member. It is a quarter-mile from my house. I asked Dedra to find a sweet girl with a pretty voice to sing one song: "Precious Memories," which was sung at my mother's funeral, and to give anybody who wanted to the opportunity to say a few words.

"You'd better keep it under some control, though," I pointed out, "because if the crowd gets bored with the eulogy, a gin game will break out." They're mad to play gin at Ansley.

I asked her to contact the Reverend Gilbert Steadham, who had been the Methodist minister when I was a boy in Moreland, to come and offer a prayer. Preacher Steadham, as country folks call their ministers, had been around when my father was battling the bottle as well as whatever it is that makes a man go crazy after two wars, and had tried his best to help him. The preacher was one of the few who never gave up on him.

"Tell him," I said, "to assure everybody I went to heaven. 'Cause there will be some doubts."

Then Dedra said I told her to buy a headstone and put it in the plot in the Moreland Methodist Cemetery and to place it next to my mother's.

"Anything special you want on the stone?" she said she asked me.

"Put my name and when I was born and died," I answered, "and then put, 'He once shot par.'"

"You really want me to put that on your gravestone?"

"I do," I said. "Do you know how many people can actually say they've shot par? Not many."

Then, Dedra said, I launched into a full explanation of the time I did, in fact, shoot par 71 at the Greensboro (N.C.) Country Club.

"Anything else?" she wanted to know.

"After the memorial service," I had gone, "throw a party. Rent a big room in a hotel somewhere, and I'll leave enough

money to have a band like the Swinging Medallions to play fifties music. And get some barbecue for everybody and lots of
booze. And set up some tables, because there will be some guys
from Ansley who will get bored with the music and want to play
gin."

"Maybe She's in a Better Place"

It never occurred to me that Melissa Segars might die.
Of course, she wouldn't die. I didn't die.

When I was there on the operating table at Emory Hospital
last spring bleeding to death during a heart operation, I needed
a miracle, and I got one. Melissa would get a miracle, too, if she
needed one. How could I get one and this precious child (she
was twenty-five and looked thirteen) not?

Melissa and her family got the call. There was a donor heart
and lung waiting for her at the St. Louis Children's Hospital. In
the wee hours of Sunday morning the family boarded a private
jet and flew to St. Louis.

Melissa would receive both a heart and lung transplant. She
would not live much longer if she did not have the transplant.

She had said to me two weeks ago, "When this is over, I want
to go on a cruise."

When she smiled, she lit up the room. When she spoke she
gave it music.

Jim Minter and Furman Bisher, two men who helped my career a hundred years ago in the *Atlanta Journal* Sports Department, first told me about Melissa Segars.

She was this young woman down in Fayette County, Georgia, where they both lived, who was dying and desperately needed the operation. But there was no money to pay for it and maybe if I would write something it would help.

I wrote a column. It helped.

The Fayette community had already been trying to raise the one million dollars necessary. And it had already responded with over half of the total.

I had lunch with Melissa at Furman Bisher's house. We exchanged a few heart surgery war stories. Melissa, like myself, had been born with heart problems.

She hit me squarely between my eyes, as she did anyone who met her. She was so tiny. She might have weighed sixty-five pounds.

She had that godawful oxygen tank she had to carry around and she had those tubes in her nostrils.

Furman's wife wanted me to see his library. We had to go down some stairs. Melissa could get down the stairs, but she was afraid she couldn't get back up again.

"We can go back out through the basement," said Furman's wife. Melissa's life was like that. Obstacles everywhere.

Jim Minter called me Sunday morning to tell me Melissa and her family had flown to St. Louis and that the operation would be Sunday afternoon.

"She wanted your home number so she could call you sometime and thank you for your help," Jim said. "Okay if I gave it to her?"

Jim told me, "Your contributions, following your column,

were running as much as $8,000 a day. God bless you for that."

Columnist Gerrie Ferris called me from the *Atlanta Constitution* Sunday afternoon. I was watching the Ryder Cup. She told me Melissa had bled to death on the operating table. She said the paper wanted a quote from me.

I rambled around and then said, "It's not fair."

The six o'clock news had all the details and they put Melissa's face on the screen. They interviewed a man in Fayette County who said, "Maybe she's in a better place."

She leaves her legacy of courage. She leaves a community that responded to her need in such an overwhelming manner that it reminds us, when we so need reminding, points of light do yet shine in the midst of so much darkness in the human soul.

She leaves me wondering what on earth I ever did to deserve the miracle she didn't get. Fairness.

Melissa is gone. For the rest of us, the dice roll on.

Goals of the Grateful

Rather than deal with what I am going to *deprive* myself of for whatever time God has been so kind to offer me as an extension on my life, I have been trying to focus on what I am going to *allow* myself to have.

I've worked hard during my life. I'm going to say that about myself. I'm not bragging, by any means. I shouldn't have worked as hard as I have. But I was ambitious. It cost me as much, or more, as it gained me. That pretty blonde I married when I was nineteen might have been my wife for twenty-seven years on July 17, 1993, had I not been so ambitious. I lost a second wife in Chicago because I worked seven days a week at that damn newspaper. I might still be with my third if I had been able to say no when somebody wanted to pay to hear me tell funny stories.

I would like to accomplish the following during my remaining years, in no particular order:

- Goof off more.
- Figure out a way to have more than six months in which to write a book.
- Get my golf handicap down to single digits.
- Attend more movies in the afternoon.
- Stay out of New York City. Stay out of most major cities.
- Cut down by at least half the number of airplanes in which I must ride.
- Stand in a clear stream in a cool place just once and catch a trout on a fly rod.
- Go back to Lugano, Switzerland, for two weeks.
- Find a church where they sing out of the old Methodist Cokesbury Hymnal.
- Visit the site of the Normandy invasion and write about how it feels to stand there.
- Get in some sort of vehicle like a Jeep and travel around writing columns about what's doing in small American towns during the summer.

- Run the middle fork of the Salmon River again, in an inflatable one-man kayak, and remember Browny Stephens.
- Avoid meetings with lawyers.
- And accountants.
- Hit anybody in the mouth who mentions the words "limited partnership" to me.
- Get rid of one helluva lot of real estate.
- See Catfish catch one damn squirrel.
- See Georgia win another national football championship.
- Buy a stock that actually goes up.
- Ride more trains.
- Not give a damn when some millionaire outfielder in an Atlanta Braves uniform misses the cutoff man.
- See a Republican back in the White House.
- Plant a garden and actually harvest my own homegrown tomatoes.
- Never wear another tuxedo.
- Never do six shows in six towns in six nights.
- Write more music with Dick Feller. (We actually got a check—a small one—because a couple of radio stations played "Grandma Willie's Yard," one of ours.)
- Write a funny novel. Any kind of novel, just to prove to myself I could do it.
- Write a book about male friendship.
- Spend August at the Greenbriar in West Virginia.
- Linger over Friday's beef tips and rice at Atlanta's Luckie Street Grill a little longer.
- Find a woman who would cook me fried corned beef that comes in a can and not call it Spam.
- Never experience a fourth divorce.
- Sleep without dreams.

- Put up a basketball backboard in my yard and shoot some hoops when I'm not playing golf.
- Call people I love more often.
- See Rock City. I've never seen the son of a bitch. Honest.
- Avoid having any more heart surgery anytime soon.

Report on the Hostage Situation

I am still being held hostage by an IV pole at Emory University Hospital. As we speak, I am plotting my escape.

There are several bags of medicine hanging atop my pole. From each bag a tube runs into a central tube that leads to a needle that is stuck inside the top of my left wrist. That is how the medicine gets into my bloodstream.

I'm not certain exactly what each medicine is. One rather large bag resembles a rhinoceros udder. It is filled with a white, milky substance.

Another has what looks like Mrs. Butterworth's syrup inside it, while a third is some sort of antibiotic substance—a sort of Orkin-Man-in-a-bag to ward off any bugs that might want to encamp in my innards.

Whither I goest, goest my IV pole, but we don't goest very far. The six steps from my bed to my bathroom is about the limit of how far Ivy and I can travel. We'd look silly at a karaoke bar singing "Don't Fence Me In" together anyway.

What's wrong with me is I'm sick. That's what my doctor said.

"You're sick," he said.

"And what's the plan of treatment?" I asked him.

"We're going to attach you to a pole until you get better," he explained.

You see, I take a prescribed blood thinner because I have an artificial aortic valve in my heart. But a few weeks ago my blood became much too thin, because I also took a large amount of a blood-thinning over-the-counter painkiller in an attempt to treat lower back pain I encountered during a venture around the country promoting and signing a book I wrote.

My blood became so thin, I bled internally, which is very dangerous and caused the most severe pain I've ever known.

Until my blood is back to where doctors want it to be, until I stop hurting, I'm stuck here with this pole. But I'm trying to make the best of it and look upon what is certainly a recently brightened side of my existence.

Yes, I'm in the hospital. But I didn't have to get the tux cleaned for a New Year's Eve party.

I've had the time to read Rush Limbaugh's second book, *See, I Told You So*, another masterpiece.

And you don't need to change underwear but every other day in the hospital.

Even more thrilling is the knowledge that 1993 is finally over. I am certain that it is. Dick Clark said so on the television in my hospital room.

We have, in fact, Auld Lang Syned that ball of personal anguish into history's waste dump and, for me, it was about time. 1993 was the worst year of the forty-seven I have lived.

In 1993:

- I had heart surgery and nearly died.
- I had more surgery to remove infected pacemaker wiring.
- I had whatever it is I have now.
- My dog died.
- My taxes were raised.
- My alma mater's football team, the Georgia Bulldogs, had a losing season.
- My favorite baseball team, the Atlanta Braves, had the best record in either league after the regular season and didn't even make it to the World Series.
- Bill.
- Hillary.

But 1993 is over. It's got to get better. *Got to.*

"Can't get no worse," friends have said.

My resolutions are few, but my determination is boundless.

I am going to get unattached from this pole. I am going to get well and get out of the hospital and stay out. When that is achieved, I am going someplace warm for a long time.

I survived 1993. 1994 has finally arrived.

Happy New Year to me.

Ode to Survival

While I was recuperating from my most recent operation, it wasn't always pleasant around me. I wasn't always nice to Dedra. Or Jordan. Or Steve. Or James. Or Catfish.

"Depression is normal," they told Dedra.

Didn't make it any easier. I need to get her a T-shirt that says, "I survived Lewis Grizzard's third heart surgery."

Survival.

There is that word again.

How did I manage it?

It was the skill of the doctors, of course. It was the skill and the great care of all the medical personnel involved in my case. It had to do with the wonderful technology of today. Oh, the magic they can weave in medicine.

They raised me back from near-dead. I was a gone goose. My heart wouldn't beat, for crying out loud. I had thirty hours' worth of operations in thirty-six. The only way I stayed alive after that was because somebody once invented the heart-lung machine.

And when I had come off that thing, Dr. Mark Connelly of the transplant team at Emory suggested those roller pumps, and I held on with those somehow.

I nearly bled to death, what was it, three times? There were those experimental drugs again.

Because I was out of it the whole time, I would have given all the credit to the doctors if nobody had told me any differently after the crisis.

They came to my bedside and said things I never thought I would hear such people of science say.

One said, "A higher power was looking after you. I still don't know how you made it."

Another said, "I now believe in miracles."

Dr. Randolph Martin said, "My friend, if you don't believe in the power of prayer now, you never will. I certainly do."

Of course. I remembered then. In the last column before I entered Emory, I had asked readers to pray for me.

But does anybody take anything like that seriously in 1993?

They do. Yes, indeed, they do.

They said they'd never seen anything like it at Emory. The switchboard, they told me, never stopped raging during my most critical times. And the messages were always the same:

"Tell Lewis we're praying for him."

My newspaper syndicate, the Atlanta papers, and the hospital received fifty thousand pieces of mail.

"Get well," the cards said. "We're praying for you."

When the news broke that I was on the transplant list, somebody said the hospital got a call from a convent in Kentucky. A nun was dying of a brain tumor. The sisters offered me the dying nun's heart.

A man is said to have called and offered his own heart.

"I don't have anything left to live for," he is said to have said. "Maybe Lewis does."

Every day I have been out in public since my surgery, somebody has come up to me and said something like "Glad to see you're doing better. My Sunday school class really prayed hard for you."

A man wrote, "My prayer group met at my house, and we did nothing for two hours but pray for you."

That has not stopped since I was out of the hospital.

Over at Lake Okonee, I was having dinner at a local restaurant. An older man came to my table, took my hand, and said, "Young man, we're sure glad you're still with us. My wife and I never gave up on you or stopped praying for you. As long as there is somebody to pray, there is a chance things will work out. Don't ever forget that."

There were tears in the old man's eyes as he walked away from me. There were tears in mine, too.

An entire family drove all the way from Louisiana to be at Emory to pray for me.

Reverend Gilbert Steadham, whom I asked Dedra to get to pray at my funeral, was with me and the family at Emory. I know he must have kept the prayer lines busy.

I even heard that former Atlanta mayor Andy Young said he prayed for me. And I try not to be very nice to politicians in my column.

Once I became aware of the efforts and the prayers of all who were involved, I began to wonder—how on earth will I ever let these people know how much I appreciate it? They had to have had something to do with the fact that I was still alive. Too many medical folk had said it wasn't all their work.

First, I am trying to answer each card, each letter, with a simple "Thank you." The *Atlanta Journal and Constitution* and King Features Syndicate are helping with that at this writing. I am grateful to them, too.

Second, I decided I would try to get a permit to hold a large meeting in the parking lot at Atlanta Stadium. What I was going to do was invite everybody who prayed for me to come. Then, one by one, I was going to hug their blessed necks and say, "From the very bottom of my heart, I want you to know I couldn't have made it without you."

I couldn't get a permit. Politicians.

So, what I did after that was write my first return column as a thank-you note. I hope a lot of people read it and know just how I feel. And maybe I can say it even better here:

For a long time, I will be asked this question: "So, how are you feeling these days?"

And it's an easy answer now.

I just say, "Loved. I'm really feeling loved."

ABOUT THE AUTHOR

There was nothing that LEWIS GRIZZARD
didn't find funny. Villard Books would like
to thank him for that as well as for this, his
final collection.

AVAILABLE FROM BAD BOOT PRODUCTIONS

VIDEOCASSETTES:

New: •Home Video: A Casual Conversation with Lewis (1991)	$14.00
•An Evening with Lewis Grizzard (1985)	$20.00

COMEDY TAPES:

New: •One Last Time (1994)	$10.00
•Don't Believe I'da Told That (1991)	$10.00
•Addicted to Love (1989)	$10.00
•Let's Have a Party (1987)	$10.00
•From Moreland to Moscow (1986)	$10.00
•On the Road with Lewis Grizzard (1985)	$10.00

COMPACT DISCS:

New: •One Last Time (1994)	$14.00
•Don't Believe I'da Told That (1991)	$14.00
•Let's Have a Party (1987)	$14.00
•From Moreland to Moscow (1986)	$14.00
•On the Road with Lewis Grizzard (1985)	$14.00

Georgia residents add 6% sales tax.
Please add $4.00 for shipping & handling.
Make checks payable to:

Bad Boot Productions
3423 Piedmont Road, N.E.
Suite 200
Atlanta, GA 30305
or fax your order (404) 266-0089

For additional information regarding previously published books by Lewis Grizzard, write to:

3423 Piedmont Rd, N.E.
Suite 200
Atlanta, Georgia 30305

The songs of Lewis Grizzard are in production and will be available on cassette soon.